European Issues in Children's
Identity and Citizenship **7**

History Teaching, Identities and Citizenship

Edited by Luigi Cajani

Trentham Books
Stoke on Trent, UK and Sterling USA

Trentham Books Limited

Westview House	22883 Quicksilver Drive
734 London Road	Sterling
Oakhill	VA 20166-2012
Stoke on Trent	USA
Staffordshire	
England ST4 5NP	

2007 © Luigi Cajani

First published 2007

British Library Cataloguing-in-Publication Data
A catalogue record for this book is available from the British Library

ISBN-13: 978-1-85856-366-4
ISBN-10: 1-85856-366-6

Designed and typeset by Trentham Print Design Ltd., Chester and printed in Great Britain by Cromwell Press Ltd., Wiltshire.

iv

Contents

European Issues in Children's
Identity and Citizenship **7**

History Teaching, Identities and Citizenship

Series Introduction:
European Issues in Children's
Identity and Citizenship

History Teaching, Identities and Citizenship is the seventh volume in
the series European Issues in Children's Identity and Citizenship.
The series has arisen from the work of the ERASMUS Thematic
Network Project: Children's Identity and Citizenship in Europe
(CiCe). This Network has brought together over 100 university
departments in 29 European states, all of whom share an interest in
the education of professionals who will work with children and
young people in the area of social, political and economic education.
The Network links many of those who are educating future teachers,
youth workers, social pedagogues and social psychologists in
Europe. The CiCe Network began eight years ago and has been supported by the European Commission's Department of Education and
Culture since 1998. We have now formed a CiCe European Association, independent of the Commission, membership of which is
open to individuals and institutions. It is now completing its third
phase of development, and planning for a fourth phase of activities
up to 2011.

These volumes have come from our conviction that the changes in
contemporary European society are such that we need to examine
how the processes of socialisation are adapting to the new contexts.
Political, economic and social changes are underway that suggest
that we are developing multi-faceted and layered identities that
reflect the contingencies of European integration. In particular, children are growing up in this rapidly changing society, and their social
behaviour will reflect the dimensions of this new and developing
social unit. Identities will probably be rather different: national
identities will continue alongside new identifications, with sub-

national regions and supra-national unions. Our sense of citizenship will also develop in new ways: multiple and nested loyalties will develop, more complex than the simple affiliations of the past. This book particularly focuses on the role played by the teaching of history in the development of identity and of a sense of citizenship. Historical consciousness and historical memory are not simply part of looking backwards, but also a way of identifying one's self and one's society for the future.

Those who teach and work with children and young people have a particular role to play in helping young people develop their own identities and understanding of society and its history, while recognising how different this might be from that known and understood by parents and grandparents.

This series is designed to discuss and debate the issues concerned with the professional and academic education of teachers, early childhood workers, social pedagogues and the like. They will need to understand the complex issues surrounding the socialisation and social understanding of the young, and to be aware of the similarities and differences in professional practices across Europe. They will need to work with young people learning to be citizens – citizens both of the traditional political entities and of the developing new polities of Europe.

CiCe welcomes enquiries from potential members of the Network and the Association. These should be addressed to the CiCe Co-ordination Unit, at the Institute for Policy Studies in Education, London Metropolitan University, 166-220 Holloway Road, London N7 8DB, United Kingdom.

Alistair Ross
Series Editor

On behalf of the editorial committee: Marta Fulop, Soren Hegstrup, Riita Korhonen, Beata Krzywosz-Rynkiewicz, Christine Roland-Levy, Julia Spinthourakis and Ann-Marie Van den dries.

Chapter Synopsis

Chapter 1: Introduction: Citizenship on the verge of the 21st century: the burden of the past, the challenge of the present

This introductory chapter briefly outlines the relationship between history teaching, collective identity building and citizenship education, from its origins in the 19th century framework of European nationalism to its present crisis under the challenge of multiculturalism, as a consequence of world-wide mass migration and of cosmopolitism. The key element of this relationship is ethnocentrism, which is a recurrent theme through the chapters of this book. This crisis can have a positive outcome, delivering history teaching and citizenship education from each other – setting the former free from political bias and able to become a critical tool in understanding present societies and their past, and the latter free from the burden of past conflicts and able to envision the future meeting the rapidly changing needs of societies.

Chapter 2: Memory, History and the quest for the future

This chapter discusses the similarities and differences between historical memory and historical consciousness and gives an outline of the basic principles constituting historical sense and meaning in these realms of human culture. It addresses different dimensions of historical culture and tackles the main issues of cultural difference, historical identity, ethnocentrism and the possibility of overcoming it.

Chapter 3: Changing citizenship, changing educational goals, changing school subjects? An analysis of history and geography teaching in France

This chapter suggests that it would be fruitful to examine not just the topics that are studied in school but also school practices, and to examine the consistencies between curriculum content, classroom practice and the expressed aims of the subject, taking account of their *epistemological frame*. The French case study is specifically heuristic, because there are parallel changes taking place in the definition of citizenship, in subject content and in school practice. The author characterises the on-going shift from a positivist view of school history and geography to a constructivist and critical view of the same subjects, and argues on its links with a new orientation towards critical and individual citizenship, and with new abilities that are expected from a reliable citizen. The chapter points at some paradoxes and tensions in the teaching of history and geography in present France.

Chapter 4: Citizenship and nationality in history teaching in post-communist Romania

The first part of this chapter presents the evolution of history education in the Romanian school system during the 1990s, with a discussion on the relationship between ethnicity, national identity and citizenship in history education in Romania. This part also discusses a poll of consumers of history education – pupils, students and teachers – on their attitudes to the goals and role of history teaching, and on the relation between history and the construction of identities and solidarities. The second part of the chapter analyses case studies of how history textbooks approach the critical moment in 1918 in Romanian history.

Chapter 5: History teaching and the educated citizen: the case of History teaching in the Greek gymnasium

This chapter introduces two questions: is history teaching and learning relevant and useful in our turbulent and exciting times and, if so, how it should be taught? Experiences from Europe and USA suggest the positive role of learning history in the development of the educated citizen, and the Council of Europe's recent recommendations describe what history teaching should entail. History teaching in the Greek gymnasium is presented against this background, focusing on recent reforms specifically in the history curriculum. These show that the new curriculum has incorporated recent developments in historical thinking and related pedagogy. Special consideration is given to identity and patriotism, the coverage of Turkish occupation in Greek textbooks, and the role of the Orthodox church in forming and preserving national identity.

Chapter 6: History and civic education teaching, identities and citizenship: a case study of Cyprus

This chapter examines the significance of citizenship education and history teaching in the history of Cyprus from the 19th to the 21st century, defining crucial time-lines in which the meaning, teaching and importance of citizenship education and history had gradually changed. The historical hermeneutic approach employed the examination of the various phases of the history of Cyprus emphasises the role of institutions, individuals and contextual circumstances that underline the official policy on citizenship education and teaching of history.

The uncertainty and the importance of the political situation in Cyprus, as well as the feeling that Greek national identity has been under threat and dispute, make policy makers, teachers and textbook writers hesitant to deal with contentious issues. Textbooks and curricula have historically been used both as a means of exercising social, economic and cultural control, and also as instruments of production and reproduction of the divisive role of education and national ideology.

Chapter 7: The contribution of history to citizen education: Historiographical analysis and reflections on teaching citizenship

This chapter presents the approach to citizenship education in Spain. It begins by examining the different profiles of citizenship in different historical periods; the influence of various historical events on the development of the concept are explained, leading to an analysis of some current challenges. The chapter then reviews the social sciences, geography and history in compulsory Spanish secondary education, and the relationship between these and citizenship education.

Chapter 8: People meet history – a Swedish television production in a medieval milieu

During the autumn of 2004, Swedish Television broadcast a reality series called *Riket – The Kingdom*. This was set in a contrived medieval environment: to create a suitable atmosphere reminiscent of the Middle Ages for participants and audience, the series was filmed at the medieval Polish castle of Grodziec. The format was a reality show, in the last episode of which one of the participants was to win the much-desired 'master-jewel'; the sub-text of the series was man's lust for power as driving force throughout history.

The series was a large and expensive project for Swedish Television, with a budget of over three million euros and a production team of over a hundred people. Accompanying the television series, the *Riket* project included a web site and a history book. On the web site viewers were able to follow the series, chat and express views about it, and also make links to books with historical references to the Middle Ages. These were intended to be used as teaching aids if teachers used the series as a starting point for history lessons in the classroom.

Riket creates an historical backdrop to tell something. The question is what? Is Riket primarily about the Middle Ages, or about people of today, about class relations or about the way society might look in the future? By using *Riket* as a springboard for the teaching of history, by working through and problemetising the messages and scenarios in a medieval costume drama, we can help our pupils to develop their historical consciousness.

Chapter 9: Leading forward: the experiences of Palestinians and Israelis in the Learning Each Other's Historical Narratives project

This chapter describes twenty-five workshops (2001-2006) in which seven Palestinian and seven Jewish-Israeli teachers developed a joint textbook, with the help of two historians and the co-directors of PRIME (Peace Research Institute in the Middle East). The joint schoolbook includes two narratives (an Israeli and a Palestinian) of nine important historical periods in their mutual conflict, covering the period of 1900-2000. The project developed as a kind of island of sanity under fire: working under severe violent conditions of asymmetry of power relations – the occupation of the Palestinian territories and the suicide bombings against Israelis. The teachers taught experts of the two narratives in their classrooms and summarised some of their pupils' reactions, as well as their own, before developing additional narratives. Some of the pupils' negative initial reactions helped the teachers express their own negative feelings, but this did not cause them to forgo their commitment to continue their joint work on writing a book that contained the two narratives. The process, described chronologically, helped the teachers realise that they must develop narratives more inclusive and sensitive to each other, more interdependent though still separate, as there is currently no chance for a bridging narrative between the two sides.

1

Introduction
Citizenship on the verge of the 21st century: the burden of the past, the challenge of the present

Luigi Cajani

History, identity and citizenship developed into a strong triad in Europe during the 19th century in the establishment of nation-states. Politicians and intellectuals gave history the task of constructing the biography of nations by inventing traditions, ethnogenetic myths and heroes (Geary, 2002), a biography which had to be traced as far back as possible into the distant past. This national biography served for the citizens to identify themselves as part of a collective body, the nation, to which they belong, mostly by birth, and to which they owe allegiance. This was the way to citizenship, a citizenship which was only exerted in the boundaries of the nation-state. This process of identity and citizenship building by history teaching is synthesised in the words of Ernest Lavisse (1842-1922), a prominent French historian:

> Moral and patriotic teaching: this must be the outcome of history teaching in primary education. ... Our very flesh and blood is at

1

stake. In other words, if pupils are not imbued with the living memory of our national glories; if they do not know that our ancestors fought for noble reasons upon one thousand battlefields; if they do not learn how much blood and how many efforts were spent in order to accomplish the unity of our fatherland and to draw thereafter, out of the chaos of our aged institutions, the laws that made us free men; if pupils do not become citizens conscious of their duties and soldiers who love their guns, teachers will have wasted their time. (Lavisse, 1885, p209-210)

In German schools, in the same years, national and dynastic pride were preached together. In 1871 the Emperor Wilhelm II addressed these words to the teachers:

Germans, and above all the citizens of the Prussian state, enjoy the great privilege to have a Fatherland and a royal house, whose history they can be proud of. (Bergmann, 1982, p195)

And in 1900 the Prussian *Kultusministerium* (Ministry of Education) prescribed the teaching of imperialistic politics:

In the upper secondary school the teaching of history [must give] to the students the clear awareness of the value of a strong fleet and of the relation between naval power and the wealth of peoples. (Bergmann, 1982, p200)

Both French and German examples show how the teaching of history aimed to instil in students' minds not only the love and pride for their fatherlands, but also the willingness to fight in future wars. The same can be said for other European states.

This nationalistic and militaristic way of teaching history was first challenged in the period between the end of the 19th century and the outbreak of the First World War, by pacifist organisations, both international, such as the Carnegie Foundation, and national, such as the Dutch association *Vrede voor Recht*, that carried out in 1910 a revision of Dutch history textbooks, underlining the strong presence of warmongering issues (Schröder, 1961, p48). In France, several teachers' associations took sides against chauvinism and militarism in school teaching, and this led to the publication of a number of pacifist textbooks. The latter, however, were either banned or had little circulation (Garcia and Leduc, 2003, p145-146).

Such initiatives of history textbook revision multiplied after the First World War. Of particular international relevance was the *Comité International pour la Coopération Intellectuelle*, which operated on behalf of the Society of Nations (Renoliet, 1999). Among the activities carried out by national teachers' associations, in France the *Syndicat National des Instituteurs* in 1926 denied its approval to history textbooks containing chauvinistic and anti-German expressions. Similar initiatives were also taken in Germany (Schröder, 1961, p51-55).

The period between the two world wars was not the best moment for such initiatives of moral disarmament. Only after the end of the Second World War did the trend become definitive and positive, and this persists until now. The main protagonists have been Unesco, the Council of Europe and, in Germany, the Georg-Eckert-Institut, which often cooperate with each other.

UNESCO aimed at a new history teaching education for peace through a world-wide vision of history, as the French historian Lucien Febvre stated in 1949:

> National history on a political basis, as is taught everywhere, will never tend to reconcile the various peoples... We must create the possibilities of a new kind of teaching, the teaching of a non-political world history, a teaching which will be, by definition, consecrated to peace. (Allardyce, 1990, p31)

We find similar proposals in a recent and highly significant UNESCO document, the report on Education in the 21st century, drawn up between 1993 and 1996 by a commission presided over by Jacques Delors:

> Worldwide solidarity also means overriding the inward-looking tendency to focus on one's own identity in favour of an understanding of others based on respect for diversity. [...] Education should therefore seek to make individuals aware of their roots so as to give them points of reference that enable them to determine their place in the world, but it should also teach them the respect for other cultures. Some subjects are of crucial importance in this regard. History, for instance, has often served to bolster a sense of national identity by

3

highlighting differences and extolling a sense of superiority, essentially because history teaching was based on a non-scientific outlook. [...] Knowledge of other cultures leads, then, to an awareness of the uniqueness of one's own culture but also an awareness of a heritage common to all humanity. (Delors, 1996, p49)

The Council of Europe acted on the European level, with the double intention of removing nationalistic bias and the negative attitudes towards other European countries from the teaching of history in member states, and of building up a new vision of history, a European one, which fits the needs of the new political project of European Union. The most intensive part of this activity took place during the 1950s, and the goal has been achieved indeed: nowadays the focus of history in the schools of many European countries has shifted from the single nation-state to Europe as a whole (Pingel, 1995, p287).

After the fall of the Berlin Wall, old and new Eastern European states joined the Council of Europe; subsequently, many of them joined the European Union. This gave the Council's activities a new impetus, with the problem of tuning the teaching of history to the new political situation (Council of Europe, 1999). Later, a major challenge was the collapse of Yugoslavia and the subsequent conflicts among the states which arose from it, which deeply influenced the teaching of history. Many international agencies considered that one of the important tools for achieving pacification of the area was the intervention of history teaching, to contrast nationalistic and aggressive trends. UNESCO organised a conference *Disarming History: Combating Stereotypes and Prejudice in History Textbooks of South-East Europe* (in Visby, Sweden, 23-25 September 1999). The Council of Europe developed textbook revision and teacher-training activities as part of the framework of the Stability Pact for South Eastern Europe, adopted by the Ministers of Foreign Affairs of the European Union in 1999 (Stradling, 2000).

The *Georg-Eckert-Institut für internationale Schulbuchforschung* (founded in 1951 in Braunschweig, in the Federal Republic of Germany by Georg Eckert as *Internationales Institut für Schulbuchver-*

besserung, and renamed after his death in 1975) has developed substantial bilateral and multilateral textbook revision, not only inside Europe, but also outside, with particular attention to conflict zones (Becher and Riemenschneider, 2000), and has also collaborated with the Stability Pact for South Eastern Europe.

This dialogue among national visions of history is a necessary first step in challenging political bias in history teaching and in promoting reconciliation between states with a common past of violence. This practice is going on in many situations. I will only mention two recent cases.

First, the group of historians from Japan, South Korea and the People's Republic of China, who wrote together an unofficial textbook aiming to present a shared vision of their common history during the 19th and 20th centuries, published in 2005 with the title *A History That Opens the Future: Modern and Contemporary History of Three East Asian Countries* [Tokyo: Kôbunken (in Japanese)]. In this case the most sensitive issue was the war crimes committed by Japanese troops in the two other countries before and during the Second World War.

Second, the establishment in 1993 of an Italian-Slovenian committee to reconstruct their common history between 1880 and 1956, a history marked during the Second World War by mass murders, deportations and population displacements on both sides, which have left a long-lasting wake of resentment. In 2000 this committee released a report where both sides recognised their mutual responsibilities (*Relazione della Commissione mista storico-culturale italo-slovena*, 2000; Slovensko-italijanski odnosi 1880-1956, 2001).

This kind of dialogue is necessary but still not sufficient to challenge the essence of ethnocentrism. These dialogues can lead to a non-aggressive ethnocentrism, which is important progress, or to a broader ethnocentrism, as in the European case, where Eurocentrism incorporates old nationalisms but still remains closed outwards: in European history textbooks the rest of the world remains on the margins and is dealt with according to when and how Europe becomes involved. The problem with ethnocentrism is both historiographical and political, because it represents a unilateral and partial approach to history, on which a collective identity is invented. Historical ethnocentrism can be overcome by a world vision of history, a vision not from the bottom, from an ethnic centre, but from the top, encompassing the human experience as a whole. A history of humanity with 'a view from the moon' (Allardyce, 1990, p40), the impressive metaphor by Leften Stavrianos, one of historians who in the 1960s opened the current season of world history research, an area which has now achieved a major status among historians (Manning, 2003; Bentley, 2005).

World history research is indeed the solution to the epistemological limits of any partial – that is 'centred' – historical analysis. But it also has educational and philosophical implications. On the educational level, world history, by shifting the focus from the ethnic or cultural group to humanity as a whole, makes an intercultural approach possible, which has become for many years a major issue in many European states, because of the increasing number of immigrants from outside Europe. On the philosophical level, world history goes arm in arm with cosmopolitism, as happened during the Enlightenment. Cosmopolitism is now in a revival phase, linked to the debate on constitutional patriotism, human rights and globalisation, as discussed in the works of Jürgen Habermas and Ulrich Beck. The essentialist vision of cultures is challenged by the analysis of Zygmunt Bauman (Bauman, 2004), and Manuel Castells has developed the concept of 'networked individualism' (Castells, 2001, p129-133) to describe the new social condition which is developing through the acceleration of communication, which dramatically loosens the bonds between the individual and a society rooted in a territory and closed by a single language.

Today the triad 'history, identity and citizenship' has conceptually shaken down, but still stands and finds support. Nationalist patterns and political bias still prevail in the teaching of history worldwide (Ferro, 1984; Procacci, 2005). The teaching of world history has been successfully established in the United States (*National Standards for History*, 1996; Lopes Don, 2003), but it has been significantly refused in Italy by historians and politicians, who consider it an attack on Italian and European identity (Cajani, 2002). The idea of the identitarian use of history is generally most strong among conservatives. Against it is the idea of a purely cognitive history, taught as a tool to understand how the world has reached its present state. This is, of course, also a major contribution to citizenship education, but from a totally different perspective than the triadic system. Every school subject contributes, with its specific knowledge, to form the future citizen's ability to take rational and well-informed decisions.

No subject is more useful than another. History's special task consists of providing students with information on the forms of past political structures and social, cultural and economical dynamics; on the historical background of current political events; on the relation between human beings and environment, a key issue for contemporary ecological reflection. On the methodological level, the comparison of controversial interpretations and the analysis of documents, fundamental in history teaching, provide students with essential skills for the exercise of citizenship. Finally, a world perspective history gives a comprehensive knowledge of the basic features of world cultures and thus helps the students to develop a multiperspective approach to social issues, to open the mind to cultural exchanges and to think of the different forms of citizenship through the local to the global scale.

In this perspective, citizenship education becomes the general goal of school education as a whole. This idea was expressed by Tullio De Mauro, Italian Minister of Education in 2000-2001, in the introduction to a school reform plan:

> In order to educate to citizenship... the school has the task to put the basic knowledge, skills, attitudes and operational capabilities, which are necessary for the progressive acquisition of social competencies in the horizon of freedom, critical thinking, democratic participation, civic-social responsibility and solidarity at all the levels of organised life (local, national, European, world-wide) in the perspective of sustainable development. (Cerini and Fiorin, 2001, p31)

To this reform plan also belonged a world history curriculum, which was the object of the fierce refusal mentioned above. This plan was never implemented: it was immediately cancelled by the Minister Letizia Moratti, a member of the Berlusconi centre-right government. The new history curriculum in the reform plan of Minister Moratti was, not surprisingly, oriented to development of Italian and European identity.

This Italian case is one of many examples of the struggle around the future of citizenship education.

The articles collected in this book aim to contribute, in many different ways, to the debate on the present and future relationships among the elements of the triad 'history, identity and citizenship'. They touch theoretical issues, the role of nationalism in the teaching of history in some European countries, the consumption of history through the mass media, and the management of conflicts through history education.

The book opens with a chapter by Jörn Rüsen, who explores and systematises historical memory and historical consciousness in the tension field between the past and the future, and then connects them with the issues of identity and ethnocentrism, proposing a strategy for overcoming ethnocentrism, based on 'the mutual recognition of differences', which also includes, in conflict situation, a practice of mutual 'mourning and forgiving'. Rüsen also challenges cultural essentialism, because cultures are not coherent units through history: the recognition that 'the specifics of a culture are ... a combination of elements that are shared by all cultures' leads then to the theoretical dissolution of ethnocentrism.

From this theoretical introduction many threads are drawn in the chapters that follow.

Roger Johansson and Lars Berggren present a Swedish case of construction of historical consciousness through a typical event of contemporary media, a reality show based on medieval history. Interestingly, this case endeavours to connect (also critically) a show with the teaching of history, which gives it a special relevance. They analyse the underlying significance of this reconstruction of the past: does it express a European historical consciousness instead of a Swedish one?

Citizenship French style, which is presented by Nicole Tutiaux Guillon, holds many interesting elements which go beyond ethnocentrism: the importance of individual identity and responsibility, the allegiance to the political system instead of a community rooted in the past. Universal values and not national tradition are considered to be the basis of citizenship. This model comes from the Enlightenment, which has inspired many current reflections on the evolution of citizenship from a national to a cosmopolitan level. But, for the past two decades, this model has been challenged by a crisis of social cohesion arising from the diffusion of socio-economic inequality, which brings a two speed citizenship. And an additional challenge comes from a vision of multiculturalism, which gives value to differences.

A similar concern for the present difficulties of citizenship is to be found in Spain. Concepción Maiztegui Oñate and Maria Jesús Cava Mesa, after reconstructing the evolution of the concepts and practices of citizenship in Spain, from the Constitution of Cadiz in 1812 until the constitution of 1978 which inaugurated the post-Franco era, analyse the problems created today by the diffusion of social exclusion.

Looking towards Eastern Europe, the Romanian case is characterised by the presence of many ethnic minorities. Mirela-Luminiţa Murgescu and Cătălina Mihalache criticise the current approach of teaching each ethnic community in Romania its own history, because it will lead to a set of mental Bantustans, unable to communicate with each other. In their opinion, it is necessary to integrate all the histories of the majority and of the minorities.

Panayota Papoulia-Tzelepi and Julia Spinthourakis, dealing with the Greek teaching of history, see a 'balanced and inclusive world history' as the way out of ethnocentrism. Nationalism, the authors show, is still very strong in the vision of history which is given in the Greek schools and, in analysing some significant topics, they under-

9

line the role played in the building up of the Greek national identity on one side by the special ties with the Greek Orthodox Church and on the other side by the negative depiction of the Turks.

The latter element is also to be found in Cyprus, an area of conflict where Greeks and Turks meet. Mary Koutselini, in her report on history education in the Greek part of the island, gives a substantial account of the situation on the other side, underlining that since independence in 1960, when Cyprus was formed as one state, education has been used separately by both communities in order to build up national identities of their own, and the situation worsened after the division of the two communities in 1974. The connection of both communities to their motherlands has been strengthened by the use respectively of Greek and Turkish history textbooks.

The Republic of Cyprus, with its accession to the European Union, is now facing the challenge of a new history and citizenship education which is able to erase negative stereotypes against the other and to accept cultural diversity under the broader umbrella of European identity and citizenship. Not an easy task, also because of the mental habits of teachers used to a nationalistic approach. A programme of teacher training following the guidelines of the Cypriot Ministry of Education and the recommendations of the European is a urgent necessity.

Many bi-communal projects are now running in Cyprus, often with international support, like the Association for Historical Dialogue and Research (www.hisdialresearch.org/). I think it useful to quote here an ongoing research on the pedagogy of reconciliation, which is being carried out by two history educators, Hakan Karahasaan, a Turkish Cypriot, and Michalinos Zembylas, a Greek Cypriot, based on a threefold strategy: first, 'relational empathy', with the mutual recognition of the suffering other; second, a multiperspective, critical and problem-solving approach; and finally, a citizenship education based on the acceptation of differences and of 'hybrid identities' (Karahassan and Zembylas, 2006).

A report from another conflict situation, that involving Israel and Palestine, concludes this book. This project, born during a moment of peace after the Oslo accord, aims to promote the mutual recognition of both parts through the teaching of the other's vision of their common history, thus making possible a dialogue which history textbooks prevent, because they generally (and particularly in this case) ignore the existence of any narrative other than their country's own. The protagonists of the project are teachers from both sides, who met not to write a common narrative, which would prove impossible for them at the present moment, but two narratives of their own, with the help of an Israeli and a Palestinian historian, in a constant dialogue, without hiding divergences and contrasts, sharp but still inspired by a common will to peace. This collective, dialectic and bottom-up procedure has resulted in two narratives which, according to the opinions of the two directors of the project, the authors of this chapter, represent respectively the opinion of two-thirds of people in Israel and Palestine. The project has continued after the ending of the peace hopes generated by the Oslo accord, has survived many recent violent conflicts, and is now entering the stage of experimentation of the two narratives in classrooms.

This Israeli-Palestinian project is important, not only as example of the practice of 'mutual recognition' pinpointed by Rüsen as a fundamental tool for starting a conflict-solving dialogue, but also as a model of an multiperspective approach to the teaching of historical issues which divide two peoples or communities.

At the present time, the idea of citizenship developed in Europe in the context of the nation-state is seriously challenged both practically, because of the increasing world-wide migrations and the following multiculturalism, and theoretically, because of the increasing awareness of global issues and the following commitment to them of many people. Without even attempting to draw a future scenario, I think that, for a fruitful management of the present crisis, it is reasonable to indicate the necessity of abandoning the original relationship between history and citizenship. This relationship has proven to be a bias for historical research, and a burden for the development of future-oriented models of citizenship, able to cope with the problems which arise more and more rapidly. Both history and citizenship will take great advantage of this mutual setting-free.

11

2

Memory, history and the quest for the future

Jörn Rüsen

Das Vergangene ist nicht tot; es ist nicht einmal vergangen. Wir trennen es von uns ab und stellen uns fremd.

[The past is not dead; it even has not passed away. We separate it from ourselves thereby alienating ourselves.]

Christa Wolf

Memory keeps the past alive and makes it an essential part of the cultural orientation of present-day life. This orientation includes a future perspective, a direction which moulds all human activities and sufferings. History is an elaborated form of memory. It reaches beyond the limits of one's own life span. It knits the pieces of remembered pasts into a temporal unit that is open to the future and which provides people with an interpretation of temporal change which they need in order to come to terms with the temporal movement of their lives.

This future-directedness of memory and history has not yet been intensively thematised and researched. There are various reasons for this. The most important (in my view) is shown by the coincidence of a loss of confidence in the Western concept of progress (at least in the minds of Western and Westernised intellectuals) and the emergence of the memory discourse in the humanities. But it is the future which demands a critical review of the two well-developed concepts of memory and history. Globalisation confronts different traditions with the thread of a clash of civilisations as a consequence of the role played by cultural memory and historical thinking in the process of forming collective identity. Are we already provided with a cultural tool to overcome domination, exclusiveness and unequal evaluation in conceptualising identity? The unbroken power of ethnocentrism in the encounter of different groups, nations and cultures (even on the level of academic discourse) gives a clear, negative answer to this question.

There is another radical challenge for a reflected future-directedness of memory and history: the heavy burden of negative historical experience (imperialism, world wars, genocide, mass murder and other crimes against humanity) presses the process of identity building into a clash and a gap – between a horrifying past and a future which stands for its opposite. What mode of understanding can contribute to a turning away from this, towards a different future? How can historical identity be liberated from suffering from a broken string between past and future?

This chapter picks up these questions and tries to find answers on the level of meta-history. By doing so, it makes the humanities responsible for the culture they work on. It thematises the logic of cultural memory and historical thinking, since the challenges they have to answer reach into this realm of principles, which concern sense criteria and basic modes of interpretation and representation. In the first two sections, 'memory' and 'history' will be discussed as basic concepts for dealing with the past for the sake of the future. The manifold dimensioning of interpreting and representing the past will then be analysed. The two sections that follow concern issues of 'doing history' which demand special attention in the intercultural discourse of today: identity and the problems of ethnocentrism. The final section gives a short outlook on the practical dimension of intercultural communication.

Historical memory

There are different modes of the discourse of history. One can first *distinguish memory from historical consciousness.* This distinction is not very easy, since both concepts cover the same field. But they thematise differently. The discourse on memory (Halbwachs, 1980; Nora, 1989; Assmann, 1992; Assmann, 1995) makes a sharp distinction between the role played by historical representations in the cultural orientation of practical life and the rational procedures of historical thinking by which knowledge of what actually has happened is gained. It emphasises the force of the past in the human mind, mainly in pre-rational or non-rational or irrational procedures of representation. It is interested in disclosing all modes of making or keeping the past present. It is less interested in the structural interrelation between memory and expectation, thus ignoring the significant role that future-directed intentions play in representing the past. (This interrelationship of memory and expectation has been clearly explicated by Husserl's and Heidegger's philosophy of temporality (Heidegger, 1980; Carr, 1986; Carr, 1984).

The discourse on historical consciousness (Jeismann, 1985; Rüsen, 1989; von Borries *et al,* 1991; Rüsen, 2001; Tempelhoff, 2003; Kölbl, 2004) includes rationality in the sense-generating procedures of the human mind. It is especially interested in those forms of representation which give the past the distinctive shape of history. Additionally, it thematises the impact of history in the future perspectives of human life.

In an abbreviated form, one could say that memory *presents* the past as a moving force of the human mind guided by principles of practical use, whereas historical consciousness *represents* the past in a more explicit interrelationship with the present, guided by concepts of temporal change and by truth claims: it stresses the temporal distinctiveness of the past as a condition for its relevance for the present. Memory is an immediate relationship, and historical consciousness is a mediated relationship, between past and present. Memory is related more to the realm of imagination, historical consciousness more to cognition. Memory is stuck to the past; historical consciousness opens this relation to the future.

But these distinctions are one-sided. It is much more useful to mediate or even synthesise these two perspectives on presenting and representing the past.

Three levels of memory

The memory discourse has brought about a very useful distinction of three different modes of dealing with the past in social life, which are also worthwhile applying to the issue of historical consciousness (Assmann and Frevert, 1999).

(1) *Communicative memory* mediates between self-understanding and the experiences of temporal change. In this medium, memory is a matter of forming generational differences. It is a field of cultural exchange in which a milieu, as a social unit with floating limits and changing memberships, shapes itself in a way that lets people feel they belong together and yet are different in the temporal dimension, in terms of their lives across different generations. Communicative memory is reflected in discussions about the importance of the historical experience of specific events and of special symbols for the representation of a political system.

(2) When there is a higher degree of selectiveness of the represented past, communicative memory becomes *collective memory*. In this form, memory gains greater stability and has a more important role to play in cultural life. People committed to the symbolism of collective memory gain a stronger feeling of belonging in a changing world. This is also an important element of social stability for a broad variety of social units, such as parties, civil movements, schools of thought in the academic field, interest groups etc.

(3) In time, this stability may lead to *cultural memory*, which represents the core of historical identity. Here, memory is a matter of rituals and highly institutionalised performances. It has its own media and a fixed place in the cultural life of a group. Cultural memory represents the political system as an entire structure and its permanence in the temporal flow of political affairs.

These three types of memory represent different levels of selection and institutionalisation with related levels of permanence and resistance to change, and long-term historical processes can be interpreted by using the hypothesis of transforming communicative into collective and collective into cultural memory. Every historical memory is changing over the course of time but, while communicative memory is fluid and dependent on current circumstances, and collective memory shows first signs of organisational or institutional permanence, cultural memory becomes an institution with a high degree of permanence (Straub, 2002).

Responsive and constructive memory

Memory can be differentiated according to different criteria, including the way in which the past is represented. In an ideal typological sense there are two possibilities: *responsive* or *constructive* (van Beek, 2001). *Responsive* memory is triggered by the intensity of a specific experience that had burned itself into the minds of the people, so to speak. The memory hurts and a quasi-autonomous force compels people to react, to interpret and to work through it. This kind of memory becomes imprinted on the mind, bringing the past into the present as a powerful and lasting image. One of the most relevant examples of such memory is the Holocaust. The dominating concept for analysing this mode of experience in historical memory is the concept of trauma.

In the *constructive* mode, the remembered past is a matter of a discourse, narration and on-going communication. Here, memory has moulded the past into a meaningful history and those who remember seem to be masters of their past as they have put memory into a temporal perspective within which they can articulate their expectations, hopes and fears.

Historical Consciousness

Historical Consciousness is a specific form of historical memory. It is rooted in it – to a great extent even identical with it – but it is also distinguished in important aspects. The specificity of Historical Consciousness lies in the fact that the temporal perspective, in which the past is related to the present and through the present to the future, is designed in a more complex way. Especially in its modern forms,

Historical Consciousness pushes the past away from the present, thus giving it the appearance of being something else. This is not being done to make the past meaningless for the present, but – on the contrary – as a means of ascribing to the past the special importance of a historical relationship. A historical relationship is determined by a temporal tension between past and present, by a qualitative difference and its dialectics and argumentative-narrative mediation in time.

The vital power of memory lies in it keeping alive the past which those who remember have experienced. The past becomes historical when the mental procedure of going back into time reaches beyond the biographical lifespan, back into the chain of generations. Thus, the future prospects of historical thinking reach far beyond the life expectancy of the individual, into the future of coming generations. In this way, the historical relationship to the past is enriched by an enormous amount of experience. Only in this specifically historical kind of memory can the weight and the significance of historical experience come into view and be evaluated. It also changes the ways of meaningfully appropriating the treasures of past experiences. These ways of appropriation become much more complex, since they can employ a wide range of narrative strategies.

The mental process of historical consciousness can be briefly described as making sense of the experience of time by interpreting the past, in order to understand the present and anticipate the future. In a more detailed and somewhat artificial manner, the basic mental procedures involved can be organised into four elements:

■ the *perception* of another time as different: the fascination of the archaic, the obsolete, the mysterious trace, the insistent memorial, and so on

■ the *interpretation* of this time as temporal movement in the human world, according to some comprehensive aspects (eg, as evidence of the permanence of certain values, or as examples of a general rule, or as progress, etc)

■ the *orientation* of human practice through historical interpretation – both outwardly as a perspective on action (eg, as the increase of political legitimacy through political participation, as the restitution of the world before its destruction, as the institution of 'true' conditions against the decline of morals) and inwardly, as identity conceptions (eg, 'We are the children of the sun,' or 'We as a nation stand for the universality and fulfilment of human rights,' or 'We belong to the communion of saints,' or 'We represent true spirituality as against others' materialism')

■ and finally the *motivation for action* that an orientation provides (eg, a willingness to sacrifice, even die or kill, for the sake of historical conceptions of national greatness, the missionary spirit, etc.). Here, historical consciousness definitely leads into the future.

In the historical culture of the public sphere, collective memory is being overpowered by a torrent of historical images. The forms of consciousness created by literacy – and, above all, the distancing effect of rationality – could quickly decrease in significance and particularly in political efficacy. The grammar of history is becoming an imagology of presentations, in which every era is contemporaneous, and the fundamental idea of a single linear movement of time is disappearing. The constitutive difference of temporality can be suspended into a universal contemporaneity which can no longer be narratively ordered. Whether there can be a specific historical order within the orientative temporal continuity between past, present and future has become at least arguable. The very term *posthistoire*, and the related discussion of a mode of life without genuinely historical interpretation (Niethammer, 1992), suggests that these questions are now open.

At the same time, there has been an immense increase in empirical access. New storage media allow new modes of historical experience, and radically call into question earlier criteria of significance. At the same time, new communication media such as the Internet allow no single, politically sanctioned decision. The abundance of possibilities and the diversity of new voices require new strategies, new forms, and new contents of historically-grounded participation and exclusion. In every case, fixed conceptions of the permanence and substance of individual and collective identity are being outstripped by the diversity of global communication, in favour of more dynamic and more open differentiations. This process provokes reactions, often expressed through these same new media, that stubbornly insist on ethnocentric distinctions.

History is founded on a specific time experience. It is an answer to a crisis, which has to be treated by interpretation. This argument can also be read the other way round: if we want to understand a manifestation of historical thinking, we have to look for the crisis, the critical time experience, that it meets.

Crisis constitutes historical consciousness. I do not think that crisis is simply an experience without any meaning. Contingency always occurs in the framework of cultural patterns of meaning and significance, but it occurs in such a way that these patterns always have to be mobilised – and sometimes even changed – in order to come to terms with the contingent event.

I would like to distinguish *three types of crises* which constitute different modes of historical sense-generation. These types are 'ideal-types' in the Weberian sense, that is, they are logically distinct but, in historiography and other modes of historical thinking and sense-generation, they occur in mixed forms and can only rarely be observed in a pure form.

(1) A *normal* crisis evokes historical consciousness as a procedure for overcoming it by employing pre-given cultural potentials. The challenging contingency is brought into a narrative within which it makes sense, so that human activity can come to terms with it by exhausting the cultural potential of making sense of temporal change. The patterns of significance utilised in such a narrative are not new. In fact, they are a re-arrangement of already developed elements, which are pre-given in historical culture. Let me give the unification of Germany as an example of this mode of coming to terms with a crisis. I suggest that a conservative German could use a traditional (exclusive) concept of national history in order to give to the challenging experience of German unification the significance of a normal crisis. From

this perspective, unification means a return of Germany to the path of national development. Such a concept would irritate Germany's neighbours and complicate the process of European unification.

(2) A *critical crisis* can only be solved if new elements are brought about through substantially transforming the pre-given potentials of historical culture. In such a case, new patterns of significance in interpreting the past have to be constituted: historical thinking creates and follows new paradigms. In the example of German unification, it could bring about a new idea of national identity which transforms traditional nationalism into a more open and inclusive one, related to the necessities of the process of European unification.

(3) A *catastrophic crisis* destroys the potential of historical consciousness to digest contingency into a narrative that is meaningful and makes sense. In this case, the basic principles of sense-generation themselves, which bring about the coherence of a historical narrative, are challenged or even destroyed. A good example of such a challenge is Saul Friedländer's remark that, looking back at the historical experience of the 20th century, one needs to ask the question: What is the nature of human nature? (Friedländer, 1998). Those principles transgress into a cultural nowhere, or even have to be given up. Therefore it is impossible to give such a crisis a place in the memory of those who had to suffer from it. When it occurs, the language of historical sense falls silent. It becomes *traumatic*. It takes time (sometimes even generations) to find a language which can articulate it.

This distinction is, of course, artificial. As with any ideal type, it is a methodological means of historical interpretation and, as such, it is contrasted to the mode of historical thinking active in everyday life. Without elements of catastrophe there would be no really challenging crisis and, without elements of normality, no catastrophic and critical crisis could even be identified as a specific challenge, not to speak of the possibility of radically changing the perception and interpretation of history. It is exactly this artificial character of my distinction which can render it useful for comparative purposes.

All three types of contingency as crisis lead to history: however, they bring about very different kinds of historical interpretation. In the first case, the narrative order integrates the challenging contingent experience. It becomes *aufgehoben* (negated and conserved at the same time) in the Hegelian sense of the word. In the second case of critical crisis, such an integration is achieved only by changing the narrative order. In the case of trauma, the challenging experience also becomes historicised, but the pattern of historical sense is shaped by it in return: it relativises its claim for a coherent narrative order, which covers the traumatic event, or it places senselessness into the very core of it. It leaves traces of incomprehensibility in the feature of history brought about by an idea of temporal change, which turns the experience of the past, the practical life activities of the present and the expectation of the future into a unity of time as a sense-bearing and meaningful order in human life. It imprints disturbance and rupture into the historical feature of temporal order as an essential cultural means of human life. It marks the limits of sense in treating the experience of time. It furnishes the coherence between experience and interpretation with the signature of ambivalence and ambiguity.

Three Dimensions of Historical culture

Historical culture is historical memory and historical consciousness working in its social context.

The interpretive work of historical consciousness and its product, the cognitive structure called history is concretely manifested in a society's *historical culture*. Historical culture is multidimensional, like every other culture. It has religious, moral, pedagogical, political and rhetorical expressions: its cognitive substance is always the knowledge of *wie es eigentlich gewesen* (how it really was). We can distinguish three basic dimensions of historical culture as ideal types, each quite different in its logic and thus accountable to different criteria of meaning.

■ the *political* dimension, concerned with the legitimation of a certain political order, primarily the relations of power. Historical consciousness inscribes these, so to speak, into the identity conceptions of political subjects, into the very construction and conception of the I and the We, by means of master narratives that answer the question of identity. There is no political order that does not require historical legitimation. The classic example, applicable to every culture and every epoch, is genealogy. Even the pure rule of law, that appeals only to the applicability of formal decision procedures, must be historically based if these procedural rules are to be plausible to the participants. Charismatic leadership cannot do without historical elements. Generally, the vehicle of political charisma will refer to the spiritual or natural forces that, within this culture, guarantee the world's temporal coherence.

- the *aesthetic* dimension, concerned with the psychological effectiveness of historical interpretations, or that part of its content that affects the human senses. A strong historical orientation must always engage the senses. Masquerades, dances, and music can all have historical content. Many older master narratives are composed in poetic form and are celebrated ritually. A formal defect can destroy the effect of such a presentation, and even endanger the world's continued coherence. Historical knowledge must employ literary models to become discursive. In many cultures, historical narrative occupies a secure place in the literary canon as a separate genre. In modern societies, memorials, museums and exhibitions are among the familiar repertoire of historical representation. In older kinds of social systems, objects such as relics, tombs, temples and churches obligate the present to the legacy of the past, indeed, they make the present, in its relationship to the future, responsible for the vitality of historical memory.

- the *cognitive* dimension, concerned with the knowledge of past events significant for the present and its future. Without the element of knowledge, the recollection of the past cannot effectively be introduced into discourses concerned with the interpretation of current temporal experience. Mythical master narratives, too, have a cognitive status, though science would eventually deprive them of it; if they did not, however, they could never have provided historical (in the wider sense) orientations. They can lose their orientative power when confronted with a science of the past that possesses a more elaborated relation to experience. Master narratives then become prosaic, as they do already in antiquity, with Herodotus and others.

Special attention should be given to the treatment of burdening, negative and (most radical) traumatic historical experiences (like slavery, apartheid, war crimes etc).

Identity and Ethnocentrism

Historical memory and historical consciousness have an important cultural function: they form and express identity (Assmann, J. 1995; Megill, 1998; Straub, 2000). They delimit the realm of one's own life – the familiar and comforting aspects of one's own life-world – from the world of others, which usually is a strange world. Historical memory and historical thinking carry out this function of forming identity in a temporal perspective; for it is the temporal change of humans and their world, their frequent experiences of things turning out different to that which was expected or planned, that endangers the identity and familiarity of one's own world and self. The change calls for a mental effort to keep the world and self familiar or – in cases of extraordinarily disturbing experiences of change – to re-acquire this familiarity.

Identity is located at the threshold between origin and future, a passage that cannot simply be left to the natural chain of events, but has to be intellectually comprehended and achieved. This achievement is produced – by historical consciousness – through individual and collective memory and through recalling the past into the present. This process can be described as a very specific procedure of creating sense. This procedure welds experiences of the past and expectations of the future into the comprehensive image of temporal progression. This temporal concept shapes the human life-world and provides the self (the 'we' and 'I' of its subjects) with continuity and consistency, with an inner coherence, with a guarantee against the loss of its essential core or with similar images of duration within the changes of subjects.

The location of the self, in terms of the territorial reality of living as well as in terms of the mental situation of the self within the cosmos, has a temporal dimension. Only through this dimension of time does the location of the self becomes fixed as the cultural habitat of groups and individuals. In situating themselves, subjects draw borderlines with others and their otherness within the locality and temporality of a common world, in which they meet and differentiate from each other in order to be subjects themselves.

Such boundaries are normatively determined and are always value-laden. In that peculiar synthesis of experiences, which determine action and purpose of what one historically knows and wishes for, oneself can be defined as remembered experience and intended goal at the same time; it is fact and norm, credit and debit, almost un-distinguished.

This is especially important for the differentiation between self and other, sameness and otherness. In order to survive in one's own world and with one's own self, and to find living here and now meaningful and liveable, each individual's own way of life is provided with posi-tive perspectives, values and normative preferences. Negative, menacing, disturbing aspects are repressed and pushed away towards 'the other', where they get extra-territorialised and liquidated.

It is part of the utility of historical memory and of historical think-ing's intentional approach to the past that whatever counts as belong-ing to one's own time and world order, and legitimises one's self-understanding, is subject to a positive evaluation; thus it is in this way generally accepted as good. In this way, negative aspects of the experience of time in relation to the world and to oneself are eclipsed from one's own world and from the inner space of one's own self; they are pushed away to the periphery and kept in that distance. The identity building difference between self and other is working in each memory, and any effort to remember is in itself an asymmetri-cal, normative relation. Ethnocentrism (in all its different forms) is quasi-naturally inherent in human identity.

This asymmetrical relationship between self and other, between sameness and otherness, makes historical memory controversial and open for conflicts. Just as the stressing of one's own group-identity will be met with consent by its members, it will be denied by those beyond the border-lines who do not recognise themselves in these time-tableaux, let alone consent to them. Degrees of such an asymmetry vary enormously: their general quality is that of tension, that is, they are always on the brink of a *bellum omnia contra omnes* among those who exclude each other in constituting their own selves. Of course, all parties usually have a common interest in preventing an outbreak of this tension. Therefore they seek and develop ways of intra- and intercultural communication in order to tame, civilise or even overcome the ethnocentric asymmetry.

Ethnocentrism is a widespread cultural strategy to realise collective identity by distinguishing one's own people from others. I use the word here in a more general sense, not in its strict anthropological meaning where it is related to an identity focused on the social unit of a tribe. It simply means a distinction between the realm of one's own life as a familiar one from the realm of the lives of the others, which is substantially different; and it realises this distinction with values which put a positive esteem on one's own group and a negative one on the other group (under specific conditions of self-criticism, it can be seen as the other way around). Masayuki Sato gives illustrating examples of cartography (Sato, 1996).

Ethnocentrism defines one's own identity by a specific distinction from the other: the otherness is placed beyond the limits of one's own life form in such a way that the value system which regulates our relationship with our own people is different from the value system we use to deal with others. We tend to attribute mainly positive values to ourselves and the contrary concerning the otherness of the other. Otherness is a negative reflection of ourselves. We need this otherness to legitimate our self-esteem (Neumann, 1985; Müller, 1987; Müller, 2000).

Identity building along the lines of this cultural strategy of ethnocentrism inevitably leads to clashes between different collective identities. These clashes are grounded on the fact that the others do not accept our devaluation; on the contrary, they put the blame of their negative values on us. The point of this deeply rooted and widely realised strategy of togetherness and separation from others, or – in brief, of identity building – is the tensional impact in its relationship between the two fundamental realms of togetherness and difference, of selfness and otherness. The clash is logically in-built into this cultural strategy. The last word in the cultural relation-ship between different communities guided by ethnocentrism will be struggle, even war in the sense of Thomas Hobbes' description of the natural stage of social life (*bellum omnium contra omnes*).

The unambiguous ethnocentricity of an historical orientation is based upon three principles:

a) Firstly, the positive and normative evaluation of one's own his-tory and the negative evaluation of the history of others (norma-tive dualism or Manichaeism of values).

b) Secondly, an unbroken continuity of one's own development from early origins to relevant projections of the future (repro-jective teleology).

c) Thirdly, a clear location of one's own positive development in the centre of history and the corresponding discriminating marginalisation of others (temporal and spatial centralism).

This general structure (understood as an ideal-type) of historical consciousness as a cultural medium of identity building can be identified in all cultures and all times. It has also determined histori-cal consciousness in Europe up to our times.

Corresponding to these three principles of ethnocentrism there are three principles for overcoming ethnocentrism:

(a) In respect to the unequal evaluation, the identity forming value system must include *the principle of equality* going across the dif-ference between self and others. The difference itself then loses its normatively dividing forces. But equality is an abstraction going be-yond the essential issue of identity: differences of engraved histori-cal experiences and obligatory value systems. If one applies the prin-ciple of equality to identity formation and, at the same time, keeps up the necessity of making difference, the logical result will be *the principle of mutual recognition of differences*. Mutuality realises equality and, in this form, equality gets the form of a balanced inter-relationship. If we attribute to this interrelationship a normative quality (which is necessary since the issue of identity is a matter of constituting values) it becomes the principle of recognition.

In order to introduce this principle it is necessary to break the power of self-esteem and its shadow of devaluating the otherness of the other. This demands another strategy of historical thinking: the necessity of *integrating negative historical experiences* into the master narrative of one's own group. Thus the self-image of a people becomes ambivalent, and this enables a people to recognise otherness. A short look at the topical historical culture in Europe will provide many examples. The catastrophic events of the 20th century are a challenge to raise this ambivalence in the historical self-awareness of Europeans.

Such an integration of negative, even disastrous and deeply hurtful experiences into one's own identity causes a new awareness of the elements of loss and trauma in historical thinking (Friedländer, 1994; LaCapra, 1994, 2001; Roth, 1995; Giesen, 2000; Ankersmit, 2001; Rüsen, 2002). New modes of dealing with these experiences, of working them through, become necessary. Mourning and forgiving could be such cultural strategies in overcoming ethnocentrism (Winter, 1995; LaCapra, 1997; Ricoeur, 1998; Liebsch and Rüsen, 2001; Rüsen, 2003; Mozes Kor, 2004).

(b) In respect to the principles of teleological continuation, the alternative is the idea of historical development, conceptualised as a reconstruction of a temporal chain of conditions of possibility. This kind of historical thinking is a gain in historicity: one definitely looks *back* into the past, and not forward from an archaic origin to the present. Instead, current life-situations and their future perspectives are turned back to the past in order to get knowledge about the pre-conditions for the present-day situation and its change into the future. Such a way of historical thinking strengthens elements of contingency, rupture and discontinuity in historical experience. Thus the ambivalence and ambiguity of the identity-forming value system in the realm of historical experience can be met.

Under the guidance of such a concept of history, the past loses its quality of inevitability. Things could have been different, and there has been no necessity in the actual development. If one employs this logic in analysing European historical identity, a remarkable change takes place: one has to give up the idea that present-day Europe and the current process of unification have been inevitable since the very beginnings of antiquity. Instead, Europe has not only changed its spatial dimensions, but its cultural definition as well. Its history becomes more open to alternatives, and this kind of historical awareness opens a broader future perspective and gives space for a higher degree of freedom in the interrelationship between future and past, which is a part of the historical feature of identity.

(c) In respect to spatial monoperspectiveness, the non-ethnocentric alternative is multiperspectivenes and polycentrism.

How to conceptualise intercultural comparison

An intercultural comparison pre-supposes cultures as the subject matter of its work. How these units of comparison should be looked at is an open question. Are there pre-given entities, temporally and spatially well distinguished? If an intercultural comparison uses a theoretical framework, one must be very careful not to start from pre-suppositions which are problematic. This can be easily demonstrated in respect of the sense-criteria which constitute historical thinking in general. These sense-criteria are an essential part of a cultural code which defines the units of comparison. Consequently, cultures can be compared along the line of their fundamental concepts, which define the forms and realms of reality and human self-understanding. So a typology of a conceptualisation is a very useful theoretical basis for a comparative approach.

Yet the danger of such a theory of cultural differences lies in its tendency to substantiate or even reify the individual cultures concerned. Their internal historicity, their manifold interferences and mutual conditioning are lost from sight. A comparison is only a statement of dichotomy, of clear alternatives: historical thinking follows either this code or another. The related forms of cultural identities appear to be special realms with clear borderlines; nothing seems to exist beyond or across the single codes. But the typology itself transgresses this borderline in a decisive step and indicates a mode of thinking which does not necessarily follow one cultural code, different from the others. A typology of cultural differences is methodically necessary as a hypothetical construct, but it has to avoid the constraints and misleading views of a concept of cultures as pre-given units and entities.

This idea of cultures as being units or entities is committed to the cultural logic which constitutes identity as the fundamental difference between inside and outside. Such a logic conceptualises identity as a mental territory with clear borderlines and a corresponding relationship between self and otherness as strictly divided and only externally interrelated. This logic is essentially ethnocentric, and ethnocentrism is inscribed into a typology of cultural differences which treats cultures as coherent units which can clearly be separated from each other.

I would like to suggest a method of using theoretical conceptualisation which avoids this ethnocentrism. *Ethnocentrism is theoretically dissolved if the specifics of a culture are understood as a combination of elements that are shared by all cultures.* Thus the specifics of a culture are brought about by different constellations of the same elements. The theoretical approach to cultural differences which is guided by the idea of cultural specifics does not fall into the trap of ethnocentrism. On the contrary:

- ■ it presents the otherness of different cultures as a mirror, allowing better self-understanding

- ■ it does not exclude otherness when one culture constitutes its own peculiarity, but it keeps it included; and

- ■ it brings about a balanced interrelationship of cultures: the people who have to deal with their differences from others become empowered through recognition and acknowledgement

Communicating differences

Intercultural communication in the field of historical culture pre-supposes comparison, but goes a step further: it brings the units compared into the movement of a discourse. This discourse is difficult, because it has no established rules. And, since it touches the issue of cultural identity, it is loaded with all the problems of ethnocentrism and the urge to overcome this.

Even when the interpretative achievements of historical conscious-ness are being brought about in the academic form of historical studies, the formative power of the normative factors of historical identity remain prevalent. Even a historiography based on methodo-logically-controlled research is determined by the political and social life of the time, and by the expectations and dispositions of the audiences. Academic historiography is ascribed to an historical cul-ture, in which the self and the other are treated differently, and evaluated as normative points of view. Thus, in this context, the questions remain: if and how the difference between and the dif-ferentiation of forms of belonging, which generally determine and socially organise human life, can be approached; and how the con-flicting dimension of ethnocentric sense-making can be tamed and overcome.

The answers to these questions may be diverse: academically, his-torical studies are obliged to enforce an intersubjective validity of their interpretative transformation of the past into a historical con-struction of belonging and difference. Intersubjective validity also here includes the principle that others can agree as much as the members of one's own group. However, such an agreement would not abolish the difference between the respective forms of belong-ing, nor the particular identity of those affected by the respective his-tories. Differences and identities are articulated and coined by this appeal to the past. So the academic truth-claims ultimately depend upon the very ways in which the procedures of creating sense in the framework of methodologically-controlled research are regulated.

Today, the quest for such a regulation is becoming increasingly im-portant. Not only mere historical differences within a common culture are at stake, as was the case in a historiography committed to the national perspective and orientation of European standards of historical professionalism. Processes of migration and globalisation have produced new constellations of intercultural communication. European countries, nations, societies and states find themselves questioned and challenged in a new way by non-European nations and cultures. They criticise the cultural hegemony of the West and forcefully intend to liberate themselves from the historical interpretations that we have imputed to them. Western historical thinking has to reflect the critique of ideology which holds that, behind the universalistic claims of validity and behind the standards of reason, there are claims for power and domination which endanger, if not destroy, the sovereignty of other cultures.

This confrontation has already caused a habit of self-criticism within western interpretations of historical thinking. But this does not mean that the established institutions and methods of historical culture have already found new ways of relating themselves to the other, or of coming to terms about their cultural differences with the other. A similar problem develops within western societies themselves in the treatment of minorities, where their cultures may be perceived as being not only different, but also as uncommon and strange. How can this otherness find a place in the way of life of the majority?

The post-modern critique of the categorical application and ideological use of a variety of modernisation models has undermined the hermeneutic tone of total conviction shown when humanities researchers declare their patterns of interpretation to be intersubjectively valid – that is, applicable across all cultural differences. However, this critique threw out the baby of cognitive validity in historical reasoning with the bathwater of eurocentrism. The result is an epistemological and political culturalism which confines its insights into the specific character of cultures, temporally and regionally, to the innate scope of different cultures, so that it has become dependent on the horizon of those cultures' own self-understanding.

As well as the immense epistemological and hermeneutical problems of such an interpretation, there is the irritation, for those who follow it when freeing the value and self-esteem of the other, of eurocentric models of otherness. They find themselves handicapped in relating the liberated other self to its own culture, so that it may indeed recognise the other. This kind of culturalism transforms cultural difference into a hermeneutic monadology that prevents intercultural communication, enabling it only at the expense of any generally accepted rules.

We therefore have to understand: how can the production of cultural and historical knowledge, which is always also the production of cultural competence, be aligned to the goal of providing future generations with the means of intercultural communication?

This question can only be answered by the practice of direct communication. The objective task of cultural orientation can only be regarded as subjectively achieved and solved when the others and we agree when we historically relate ourselves to them, and *vice versa.* At that point, the mutual consensus of selfness and otherness has been achieved in historical self-realisation. (Of course, this is not conceivable as a task to be accomplished once and for all, but only as an open and ongoing process. The ever-recurring time-experiences from everyday life, from struggles for power, from collisions of interest and from the unintended side effects of our own actions and the reactions of others, call for a continuous effort to historically position oneself and to understand the self-understanding of others.)

The many voices contributing to this debate may easily be combined into a general agreement on furthering progress in conceptualising historical thinking as a medium of identity building, determining the otherness of others and relating this otherness to the self: *the decomposition of western historical thought* already in progress, its deconstruction into elements and factors to be further differentiated diachronically, needs to be continued. The pregnancy of cultural difference is decreasing with the deconstruction of the western special character of historical thinking into a complex constellation of factors, each of which is not at all culturally specific,. But this does not mean it is dissolving into a *pot-pourri* of historical sense-

33

creations, lacking the contours of an identity building self-esteem. On the contrary: the self-esteem achieves greater clarity within the complexity of the constellation in which it appears. At the same time, the mutual perception focuses on the fact that what is different about the other is composed of elements that also belong to oneself.

Together with the decomposition of western peculiarity, the special characteristics of non-Western forms of historical thinking and historical culture must be outlined; they should be made visible as peculiar constellations of general factors in the creation of historical sense. Without the perception of the other, the narrow-mindedness of historical attitudes is strengthened.

However this necessary research is carried out, its results would be weakened without a critical rethinking of the decisive questions and interpretations that make other traditions and interpretations comparable. At the very point where they could objectify and intellectually support intercultural communication, without theoretical reconsiderations they would hamper it.

Considering the urgent problems of cultural conflict in an age of globalisation and increased migration, such a use of theoretical reflections and empirical data, should take place in direct discussion of our own as well as of other traditions and contemporary forms of historical thinking. The current features and forms of academic discourse do not yet correspond to these imperatives: too often the respective experts still talk without giving them a voice in this discourse. But that can be changed.

3

Changing citizenship, changing educational goals, changing school subjects? An analysis of history and geography teaching in France

Nicole Tutiaux-Guillon

It is currently asserted as common knowledge that teaching history in schools contributes to the development of identity and citizenship. Similar outcomes are asserted or assumed for other subjects such as geography, literature, the social sciences and economics. Such claims usually link school subjects with identity and citizenship through the subjects' curricula and the ethnocentric attitudes, political values and nationalism that these bear. This chapter suggests that it would be more fruitful to examine not just the topics that are studied but also school practices and the consistencies between curriculum content, classroom practice and the expressed aims of the subject. In adopting this approach, I draw on the conception of the *paradigme pédagogique*, borrowed from studies in the history of education. This concept is used to analyse the school subjects of history and geography teaching in France. This case study is specifically heuristic, because there are parallel changes taking place in the definition of citizenship, in subject content and in school practice.

Citizenship French style: characteristics and implications for school

Citizenship in France does not refer to religious or ethnic culture or belonging, but only to a political identity. This kind of citizenship is – it is said – open to all, provided that s/he agrees to and accepts the underlying political values. This approach is theoretical, because to become a citizen it is necessary to get French nationality, and the degree of difficulty in doing so depends on the international, national and sometimes local context. Simultaneously, it is taken for granted that a French citizen belongs to only one legitimate political community: the national. In political life, any other sense of belonging – whether of gender, class, religion or regional culture – is said to be private, and specifically in politics subordinate to the sense of national belonging. All French citizens have to be able to separate their identities as citizens from aspects of their identities that are rooted in their personal histories and communities. When thinking and acting in political life, responsible French citizens must break away from their private identities.

The word *communauté* in French has a pejorative meaning: if they were politically active, communities would threat the body politic, personal freedom, and the liberty of mind and judgement. Citizenship is thus both national and individual, without an intermediary between state and citizen. Personal and social differences are subsumed or hidden by French identity. In political debate, legitimate argument refers to general common interests (incorporated as *l'intérêt de la France ou des Français*) and not to any interests of the communities, or to conflict and negotiation between them. This is true not only in mainstream political life, but also in politics in the media and even bar-room politics.

It is therefore seen as necessary that, as well as private cultures marked by gender, class, religion and region, all citizens share the same common culture that transcends every specific culture. In the French political tradition, culture is the basis for *citizenship*, more than for *nationality*. As an example of this, politicians in the French Revolution and the later Third Republic justified the eradication of regional languages and dialects by claiming the equality of rights: even the poorest citizens should learn the French language so that they could understand political debates and defend their rights. The common culture contributes to political and social bonds, and shapes the nation, not only or even mainly because a nation is rooted in its culture, but – in the traditional French conception – above all because a nation is a political construct that is based on collective agreement.

As in any culture, this so-called French culture is a mix of diverse traditions, including foreign ones. But French culture is perceived as being particularly grounded on universal values such as human rights, democracy and *laïcité*, and on universal knowledge. The claim is that this is not an alienating culture, but one that liberates: private and specific identities are limited and locked in the mind, because they favour tradition over modernity. French culture, thus defined, is linked with democracy. This position – and its implications for the content of schooling – has been criticised as ethnocentric and as oppressing social class identities, regional identities and migrants' identities, especially by leftist intellectuals during the 1960s and 1970s, and more recently by feminists.

Such a conception of citizenship and of the culture necessary for the body politic is consistent with the conception of the school as the place where one learns scientific content – universal knowledge – and where one learns to understand the contemporary world. This has been true for subjects such as history and geography since 1902. By the 1990s, even though the contents of the subjects were less centred on France, the goals remained the same. In 1995, the senior chief inspector of schools for history and geography asserted that teaching and learning history contributed to culture and to free thinking (Borne, 1995).

School knowledge in history and geography is reputed to be objective and true. School is supposed to substitute objectivity (however imaginary this might be) for individual subjectivity, stereotypical thinking and communitarian or sectarian points of view; this is just as French citizenship acts to release citizens from their private interests and prejudices. Objectivity is assimilated in scientific truth. The school passes on a common culture that is taken to be universal and legitimate, because all academic subjects are seen as scientific. This approach, shaped by the Enlightenment and by Positivism, is still commonly held today. Teachers generally assert that they must be neutral and objective, and that they must not present a point of view. They feel that they must avoid commitment and giving opinions about the themes that they teach. Audigier (1993) characterised traditional school history and school geography as being ruled by the intention to elaborate a consensus, by the claim of passing on scientific results, by the belief that school knowledge was reality, and by rejection of anything that might split society – including politics. Since the Third Republic, most teachers have regarded the good citizen as an enlightened citizen whose culture is grounded in scientific truth.

Teachers are thus confronted with a paradox: they claim objectivity or neutrality, and therefore have to avoid passing on values, even democratic ones; but by doing so they cannot promote human rights and republican values, which are part of their official social mission. There should be no social meaning to their teaching.

Recent and present changes in the conception of citizenship

The 1960s and 1970s were marked by decolonisation, by criticism of ethnocentrism, by denunciations of the marginalisation of regional cultures – and by misgivings and doubts that school played any part in the formation of responsible citizens. School was presented as mildly oppressive, and the contents of the subjects taught as bourgeois and centred only on France. The social sciences developed a critique of the role of schools in social reproduction, however much this might be masked by a pretence of fostering a republican elite. The social sciences, including history, also criticised the nationalistic element in curriculum content as alienating and a threat to peace. Tradition in any form became suspect, as did authority. School culture was no longer seen as being liberating or politically relevant.

Several school subjects, including history and geography, were revised at this time. It was thought less important to educate citizens and more important to develop producers and consumers, and to extend students' abilities and skills. Civics was dropped from the secondary school curriculum. Audigier (2003) links these changes to a growth of individualism. Providing students with a sort of intellectual tool-box (basic concepts, methods, core dates and locations) would enable them to develop their own meanings about the world:

> *Munir chacun de quelques moyens pour qu'il comprenne le monde et qu'il lui donne lui-même sens, peut être interprété très positivement comme l'affirmation d'une liberté enfin conquise sur une citoyenneté trop souvent construite sur l'obéissance; mais privatiser ainsi le sens peut aussi être interprété comme une démission collective et un abandon des jeunes générations aux logiques marchandes et communautaires.* (Audigier 2003, p210)

> [To provide the individual with the means to understand the world and all that this implies can be viewed very positively, as the ultimate assertion of freedom in a context in which citizenship was all too often founded on simple obedience; but to make this a private or individual concern can also be interpreted as collective resignation, abandoning the younger generation to the logic of the market]

At the same time, much attention about teaching focused on methods, new media, and on the basic contents considered to be necessary. Any reflection on meaning, values, attitudes or on the political goals of teaching history, geography or other subjects was minimal (Lenoir, 2000; Tutiaux-Guillon, 2004).

Several enquiries in France, from the 1980s onwards, reported growing indifference to politics, an increasingly critical view of politicians and political debates, and a weakening attachment to collective values. The media report violence and incivility amongst the young and in schools. Traditional culture became less shared, and was partly substituted either by a more global culture or one that professed a community culture. Teachers and politicians denounced these changes as representing a crisis in social cohesion and a danger to democracy; in fact the political philosophy on which French democracy is based was (and remains) rather blurred.

39

These changes in the nation-state also entail questions about the sovereignty of the citizen. As in the rest of the European Union, most current laws in France integrate international standards into national norms. National defence is now hardly recognised as a citizen's right and obligation; it is forgotten that this was a leftist republican tenet in the 19th century. The spread of multinational firms challenges the powers of the state. European citizenship, coupled with a commitment to regional and local projects, weakens the traditional link between the French citizen and nation-state. The meaning of citizenship – and particularly the relevance of its French definition – is a matter of\question. Is it still appropriate to represent the state as the principal arena for politics or the economy, when the European Union and the regions so successfully present alternative forums?

The desire to give women a larger role in politics has led to legislation for affirmative action, requiring political parties to nominate equal numbers of female and male candidates, or to face a fine. The right of non-EU migrants to vote in local elections has been discussed and, in some cities, foreigners participate in consultative assemblies. Both of these measures construct social categories – women and migrants – as political categories, breaking with the abstract conception of the citizen. Changes in the practice of citizenship are also clear: most young people do not and will not actively participate in political parties or trade unions, but they will actively engage in particular marginal anti-establishment movements. They take part in social and humanitarian activities, at local and global levels, and demonstrate for their values, for their own rights (for example as students), for migrants' rights, for human rights and against the extreme right. The conception of citizenship is moving from that of an obedient citizen towards critical citizenship; the emphasis has shifted from the general interest towards greater personal responsibility and individual freedom.

It is more difficult now, after the criticisms raised in recent years, and the recognition of social exclusion arising from homeless and of long-term unemployment, to accept the principle that all French citizens are equal to each other. Remarks are frequently made not just to a two-speed society but also to two-speed citizenship: can someone without work or a home be an effective citizen? At the same time, society strongly stresses the actualised autonomy of the individual, setting this as a goal for education. This weakens the differentiation between private and public space, in the same way as some new attitudes and behaviours such as the use of cell phones. But it is the separation between public identity and values and private identity that is, as has been argued, the fundamental basis for French-style citizenship. The limits between being human and being a citizen have become blurred, so the narrow political definition of citizenship is less acceptable as a legitimate term. This individualism questions trust in collective values and the right to transmit these to young people.

Teachers are not convinced that promoting democracy and human rights is part of their history and geography teaching. Newer teachers are not convinced that society necessarily shares the same values – even a value of individualism. The role that values play in linking groups and individuals together, and in planning a common present and a common future, is often forgotten. This can be contrasted with the debates on issues such as sustainable development, where underpinning values are very explicit. Developments like this may be a general movement in western societies (Laville, 2001).

Many members of society also regard multiculturalism as cultural and social progress. At very least, the cultural variety of our society is explicitly approved. Whilst traditionally the French were indifferent to differences, there is now a greater sensibility of differences, and affirmative action is seen as legitimate form of progress. The right of foreigners, who have civil, social and economical rights, to have the right to vote because they live and work in France, can now be considered a matter of debate. The idea that citizenship is best if based on universality has been damaged; respect and relativism have become entangled.

These questions, doubts and changes are inevitably reflected in the curriculum. Educational officials debate what are the relevant educational goals for the 21st century: education for which citizenship?

For which collective identity? Is it relevant or necessary to support plural or collective identities? Education in relation to which territory? What is the place for cultural diversity, or for a universal culture and values? How should education develop the competencies necessary to take part in public debates? How should schools teach tolerance and being open to others? Which values are absolute, on which there can be no compromise? How can schools integrate pupils without assimilating them? If citizenship is changing, then must the school be adapted – or must it resist change, acting as a breakwater?

Citizenship as a goal for school subjects

In French education, the disciplines of history, geography, social science, economics and experimental sciences all aim at developing citizenship. This goal is officially prescribed, and generally written as a preamble to the curriculum: the contents of these disciplines are thus presented as knowledge that is useful or necessary to become a responsible citizen.

History teachers regard history both as a common cultural inheritance that shapes the present world, and as a directory of counter-examples that may suggest both reflection and action. Knowledge of history could avoid the repetition of past crises and crimes. When interviewed by researchers, teachers often mention this civic role for school history: their main intention is no longer to sustain national glory, but to support human rights and tolerance (Lautier, 1997; Tutiaux-Guillon *et al,* 2005). This consensus could be seen as a mixture of commonsense and of conformity to official curricular expectations.

Choosing a definition of citizenship has consequences for the prescribed curricular contents. In France, where the relationship between citizen and state has been direct and strong, the State was given the largest place in the history and geography curricula. Analyses of French textbooks point out that the State is much more in evidence than the Nation (Audigier, 1998). In recent decades, politicians, sociologists and even teachers have questioned the ability of school to integrate youth, and specifically young people of immigrant descent, into French society and the body politic. The response in 1985 was to prescribe more emphasis on specifically French history, geography and civics. By 1995, the new curricula for middle schools emphasised common cultural references, largely traditional French but also partly European, partly Mediterranean, and a few American. These references are comparatively new, and are adapted to reflect current French/European/Western society. They are officially prescribed as a contribution to collective memory and identity. The same development is also clear in the curriculum for literature, where more space is given to non-French authors. Another example might be that, in some elements of history, greater focus is given to women, reflecting political affirmative action. But, in my opinion, the most striking change is seen not simply in the content, but in the whole functioning of history and geography teaching.

In this analysis, I draw on Chervel (1998) and Bruter (1997) for their definition of a *paradigme pédagogique*: this concept explains a specific consistency in educational goals, contents and teaching practice that is characteristic of a specific subject during a specific period. The *paradigme pédagogique* may be explicit in official curriculum prescriptions, but it may also implicitly underlie effective teaching. In my view, 20th century education was largely ruled by a positivist *paradigme pédagogique* and the last decade of that century and the first years of the 21st were marked by the emergence of a new *paradigme pédagogique* that I would describe as critical and constructivist.

The positivist *paradigme pédagogique*

My analysis is based on an examination of official documentation and on studies of effective teaching (eg Tutiaux-Guillon, 2004; Clerc 2002; Héry, 1999; Tutiaux-Guillon and Mousseau, 1998; Tutiaux-Guillon, 1998; Audigier, Crémieux and Mousseau, 1996). The positivist *paradigme pédagogique* was characterised by:

- ■ presenting school knowledge as an encyclopaedic truth about the world and the past; in which knowledge was mainly factual and enclosed

- teaching through lessons in which the teacher expounded (from the 1970s often through a lively and attractive dialogue with students), supported by documents: students were expected to reproduce the content and to imitate the organisation of the teacher's presentation

- educational goals that centred on acculturation and on adherence to republican and democratic values, in the belief that the good citizen was guided by scientific knowledge and by reason

The place devoted to concepts, interpretative models and history/ geography scenarios in such traditional teaching, was low; and there was also rather low emphasis given to competencies in history, though little more was given in geography. The best stock of knowledge to understand the world was seen to be a good directory of facts. Pictures, photographs and maps were presented as reliable mirrors of reality. The account of the teacher was taken to be a reliable account of reality. The interpretations of historians and geographers were presented as facts rather than as interpretative judgements, even in upper secondary school and even though this is done in other subjects (such as economics, sociology and the experimental sciences). Criteria to validate historical or geographical analysis and interpretation were not presented. History or geography lessons opened windows on reality, that gave students a 'truer' picture of the world and the past than did the mass-media or public opinion.

Teachers attempted in lessons to cast themselves as neutral and objective, steering clear of expressing any point of view that could be considered as unscientific, and avoiding social or scientific controversies (Tutiaux-Guillon, 2000). Students were expected to keep to the facts and to avoid personal opinion. School knowledge was presented as being independent of the teachers, in the same way that scientific truth was supposed to be independent of scholars. Even if the teachers were aware that they were selecting the knowledge (necessary and possible to pass on to students), they rarely expounded or explained their choices to students, and preferred to let them believe that what was taught was reality. The canon – called *vulgate* by Chervel (1998), was much the same from one classroom to the other, even if the curricula were more vague (Audigier, 1996; Audigier, Crémieux and Mousseau, 1996; Tutiaux-Guillon, 1998; Tutiaux-Guillon, 2000; Clerc, 2002). Curriculum contents were presented through general titles, such as *The Byzantine Empire*, or *The Maghreb*, with general comments (in these two examples, 'two aspects are to be stressed: the Roman inheritance and Greek Christianity and its expansion', and 'stress belonging to both the Mediterranean world and the Muslim world, the links with Europe, the contrast between coasts/interior/desert and demography. Such an approach induced a sense of ill-ease when scholarly knowledge was seen not to be consensual.

Teaching methods were rooted in the scientific practices of the late 19th and early 20th century: the analysis of reliable documents to find the true facts; the close observation of landscapes and maps to find the true relations between human society and nature; empirical reasoning; the exposition of so-called facts, truth or reality, omitting the processes of research and argument (Orain 2000). The vigilance over revisionist allegations renewed this stress on facts, truth and reality, and this was probably reinforced by anxieties about increasing relativism (each to his/her own truth). Teachers who were interviewed stressed this latter point. Consequently, when they select support materials for their lessons, they choose realistic documents in preference to any other, even a movie, rather than an historical source (INRP, 1989; Poirier, 1998). Realism is of core importance, so a critical approach to such documents is often lacking.

The stress on truth in traditional teaching does not give many opportunities to students to reflect or to reason. Their opinions, experiences and personal lives are not of interest in the history or geography classroom: they learn that in secondary school they must separate their private knowledge from the universal knowledge they are taught. It is said that students are too young and inexperienced to establish historical or geographical truth. They must recognise it in the teacher's talk: they must adhere to this, and possibly contribute to it with details from documents, being active listeners rather than knowledge producers. The classroom order of quiet, silence, individual work and a concentration on reading and listening is underpinned by stressing the teacher's intellectual authority as a master of truth. This adherence results in acculturation and knowledge-based science, and thus results in an obedient citizenship. Nevertheless, over recent decades students who have undergone such instruction have demonstrated their opposition to various governments and have sometimes fought the establishment! Teachers often argue that passing on a uniform school culture also passes on a culture that guarantees some social equality: for them, academic truth is not only a basis for understanding the world, but also a response to human rights. As Condorcet (1792) asserted, knowledge is the soil for democratic citizenship.

A weakened paradigm

The positivist *paradigme pédagogique* has ruled the development of history and geography as school subjects for a century: it was consistent with both the republican and the positivist conception of French-style citizenship. But it has been weakened since the 1960s because the civic and ethical goals that are part of it have been weakened – in the teachers' convictions, if not always in the official prescriptions.

We know relatively little about effective teaching in secondary school before the 1980s: our sources are scarce and not robust, often being recollections and comparisons to present-day teaching (Héry, 1999). Several recent studies have concluded that teachers distrust the stated educational goals of history and geography teaching, and that they effectively avoid them in their teaching (Tutiaux-Guillon, 1998; Tutiaux-Guillon, 2000; Tutiaux-Guillon *et al,* 2005). During the Third Republic the educational role given to the analysis of documents was to train young people to analyse concrete situations, to select relevant and reliable data, and to make judgements. While this might still be practised in other subjects, it is no longer in history or geography, except in particular innovative teaching/learning contexts. Even critical approaches to documents are now rare. Lautier has shown that the same teachers who approved the civic role of school history were disturbed when asked how they teach *for* democracy: most hesitated, and recalled content *about* past democracy. Their main goal was to pass on information and let the students judge for themselves (Lautier, 1997).

Even in the area of human rights, militancy is uncommon: teaching about genocide is supposed to be enough to develop a commitment to equality and antiracism. Teachers – particularly newly-trained teachers – do not see the contents and the practice of their teaching in the light of even the prescribed ethical or civic goals; some explicitly reject such goals. This is consistent with individualism: each person is free to selecting his/her values, but must keep them private, because public collective values are thought to alienate (Bauberot, 1997). Teaching a common culture or passing on values (even democratic ones) is often taken for indoctrination. Sensitivity to nationalism and to hidden bourgeois cultural values, developed during the 1960s and 1970s, is still strong. Some teachers when interviewed deny being nationalists, as if nationalism was in some way shameful; perhaps they feared being associated with far-right nationalistic and xenophobic political movements.

Most research on teaching and learning controversial or political topics (such as the Nation or Europe) focuses on knowledge and method, omitting values and affective attitudes. Of course, the questions proposed in such research, and in textbooks and official documents, *do* reflect values. Thus Sourp states that the geography textbooks for the third year of secondary school interpret European space either through the opposition between diversity (= fragmentation, = disorganisation) and organisation (= consistence, = cooperation) or through the basic opposition between division and unity. The geographical explanation thus legitimates the European Union (Sourp, 2002).

One could easily find analogous examples. But these values are discreet, implicit and clandestine. Clerc shows that school culture in geography hardly questions the social relevance of knowledge or the educational goals of introducing, suppressing or maintaining such topics and methods (Clerc, 2002). This could also be said of school history, even if the justifications are more common.

47

Some interviews drawn from two different studies confirm these assertions. In one, teachers stressed that the civic goals of history or geography should be borne in mind: one has to study France because students live and will continue to live there. By study they meant delivering factual information on France and fostering a critical attitude towards the mass media. But they did not mention the responsibilities of the citizen, the questioning of authorities in charge of development, or collective identities, even when based in history. Identity meant individual identity. Nor did they suggest that present preoccupations could influence historical research or historical content in school. They said studying history was necessary to explain present events and to act, but took for granted that understanding the present world and acting in it was a natural outcome of knowledge. In some interviews, there was no reference to citizenship and, in most, references were blurred, and citizenship was only referred to as critical thinking and, sometimes, political awareness. Collective freedoms, citizens' rights and obligations, and political commitment were not mentioned. In 1993, Douzant-Rosenfeld stated that, for history and geography teachers the civic role of geography was missing: those teachers whom she asked about educational goals rated 'forming a citizen' and 'doing a political job' far below 'understanding problems' or even 'travelling' or 'developing one's personal culture'. Similarly, sociological enquiries about secondary teachers' professional identity do not give any significant role to educational goals (Lautier, 2001; Barrère, 2002).

When history and geography teaching is student-centred, and with active pedagogy, students are expected to assimilate knowledge and to practice methods. They are never expected to display their competencies as citizens or as social actors, except in particularly innovative situations, or when they are reputed to be culturally deprived and possibly poorly integrated into society (Colomb, 1999). Teacher-centred lessons usually have educational goals that cannot be detected. In these subjects – as in others – teaching is routine, without any ethical resonance, and educative actions that might have an ethical resonance are swiftly transformed to become practical tools (Sarreméjane, 2001).

The critical and constructivist *paradigme pédagogique*

From the 1990s, the Ministry of Education and various conferences have urged teachers to centre their practice on the student, and to change their contents and practices to fit either academic research progress or new educational goals (for example, a positive attitude towards cultural diversity). Some timid and marginal changes have been implemented by institutions. These were linked to political and cultural evolution, and to the uncertainty about the type of citizenship that will be relevant for 21st century France. These new practices were also linked with an epistemological preoccupation of questioning relevant content. Because the world is not organised into subjects, how can school subjects develop a better understanding of the world and more efficient action? If opinion and experience have no place in the classroom, *how* can they be influenced by what is taught? If students only have to adhere to truth, to learn and to reproduce, how can they become critical citizens? And how do school subjects really contribute to citizenship education?

The list of changes that have been suggested, prescribed or encouraged recently might seem to be a jumble: case studies in geography and history, with special emphasis on actors, stakes and conflicts (for example, conflicts and problems over water in the Middle East); topics about acute social issues (such as industrial risks, conflicting memories or affirmative action); interdisciplinary practice; stress put on concepts as well as facts; non-fatalistic views of the past, stating the choices to be made and the hazards; multiple perspectives and the multiple significance of the same source, and so on. Each of these represented a break from the tradition in school history and geography.

Traditional teaching methodologies are also strongly questioned in the official guidance: even though each teacher may still choose his or her preferred methodology, most traditional practices are dismissed as inefficient. The guidance promotes active pedagogy and recommends avoiding passing on knowledge as established truth. Student reasoning should be the core of teaching practice. Teachers are to organise moments when the students will write, argue, discuss a file of documents, and not just listen to the teacher and find bits of information in the documents.

The ability to argue has become a goal of history and geography teaching since the late 1990s, explicitly as a component of citizenship, which is new: '*forme élaborée de l'expression, la capacité à argumenter donne du sens à l'effort personnel exigé des élèves ainsi qu'une dimension concrète aux finalités civiques et culturelles de l'enseignement*' [to elaborate expressions and form arguments gives a sense of personal achievement to students and a concrete expression to the civic and cultural aims of teaching] (Ministry of Education, 2000 at www.education.govr.fr). Debating is encouraged as legitimate as the traditional lecture, from the elementary school to *baccalauréat*. Examinations for secondary education have, since the late 1990s, included the ability to write and argue a text, associating knowledge with relevant analysis of imposed sources and critical thinking. These tests are rather different from traditional ones, which would only demand clearly organised knowledge.

Denier, an inspector and a researcher, showed the change to be drastic: the responsibility for personal reflection moved from the teacher to the student. Students are now presumed able to have an historical and geographical point of view about the world. She drew a parallel to the epistemological changes that recognised the importance and relevance of subjectivity in the social sciences, and concluded that students were required to develop historical awareness and become citizens for the world that they would be responsible for (Denier, 2002).

In France there is a free market for textbooks, without even recommendations from the Ministry, but publishers ensure textbooks match the prescribed curricula and what they imagine to be teachers' expectations. Teachers choose textbooks in each school, often for four or five years. In 1996, three out of the eight textbooks published for the fifth year of secondary education included sections linking present developments and issues to past events or choices. Some of these concerned how contemporary society might question the past, while others pointed out that knowing about the past might be a resource for deciding on current action. By 2001, all except one of the publishers had abandoned this, perhaps because citizenship in secondary schools was by then allocated to the separate subject of civic, legal and social education. The following table gives examples of these interesting attempts to link history teaching and citizenship.

Publisher	1996	2001
Bréal	'past and present'	'past and present'
	a stress on social or political problems: a characteristic from a past situation is transposed to a present one	a stress on evolution: what are the consequences and the heritages from the past?
Hatier	pages 'main points to remember', including 'from past to present'	Nothing
	questions about how the past can help explain present situations	
Magnard	'debate'	Nothing
	transposing to the present a question arising from a situation in the past that has been studied earlier	
Belin, Bertrand-Lacoste, Nathan Hachette, Nathan	Nothing	Nothing

Each of these textbooks has roughly the same title: *Histoire, classe de Seconde*; the authors are numerous, so the core reference is to the publisher. Each reference can be inferred from the table as follows: *Histoire, classe de Seconde*. Paris : Breal, 1996.

I would interpret these changes, institutional and publishers', as echoing the changes and questions about citizenship. Democratic abilities somehow become abilities to judge, to achieve a compromise (a compromise both of expert knowledge and of social values), to accept diversity not as a difficulty but as a component of any society. Changes are limited, because students are not required to reason dialectically, or even to confront contradictory sources or to elaborate a problem by themselves. But the new citizen-in-the-making is more critical, better able to take part in democratic debate, more aware of conflicting interests and social positions. S/he should be a reasoning citizen, aware of the difference between common sense, media information and scientific knowledge. At the same time, s/he will understand that acute social problems cannot be solved by science only, and that politicians are responsible for choices.

My inference of such an ideal is derived from the official texts; but they do not detail this in an explicit manner, apart from requiring critical competencies. Perhaps the school system is missing a potential clear political and social project? I suggest that this development is evidence of the emergence of a new *paradigme pédagogique* that I call constructivist and critical. This paradigm is characterised by:

■ new types of pedagogic practice: debates, enquiries and research, interactivity, differentiation of learning and of the learning process

■ a new status for school knowledge: more open to the lived-in world, presented as constructed knowledge that can be debated, providing answers to problems and as interdisciplinary and plural; and

■ a new understanding of citizenship, tending to the universal: more critical, rooted more in a diversity of identities, more active, and perhaps as social as it is political

In a school ruled by the positivist *paradigme pédagogique*, one learns to be a citizen by acquiring and building up knowledge that is expected to guide one's later judgements and actions. In a school following the constructivist-critical *paradigme pédagogique*, one learns to be a citizen by developing the intellectual competencies thought to be at the core of critical and aware citizenship. This construct-tivism is a paradigm for knowledge and pedagogy: it is also a para-digm for learning, particularly of learning to be a citizen.

This paradigm – even if my interpretation is correct – is nevertheless still marginal. It underlies many professional publications, especially those of researchers of pedagogy and didactics, and is an implicit reference within teacher training, even though the implications for citizenship have yet to be worked out. But teachers have to move from the position where they are masters of truth and authority to a more blurred position, in which only a strong epistemological back-ground and a firm commitment to these educational goals can give reassurance. This is a very real difficulty.

Conclusion

Beyond the example of France that I have developed in this chapter, I suggest some more general conclusions. An examination of the *epistemological frame* of school knowledge is a more efficient way to characterise the link between citizenship and school subjects than a more traditional analysis of the topics that are studied. Contents that are apparently identical may be taught either in a traditional positivistic way or in a critical constructivist manner: but the effect of each approach on the students' abilities and their relation to the world and the past will be as different as the status of knowledge. From the reverse perspective, the definition of citizenship and general educational aims strongly influences not only the contents, but also the status of school knowledge and the practices that are en-couraged or prescribed. Those times when definitions of citizenship are changing offer good case studies for such research. For example, the introduction of European citizenship as an educational goal introduces not just specific topics relating to European culture and debates, but also possibly specific practices (which ones?) and dif-ferent *types* of knowledge – more comparative, more multi-scale, more multi-perspective. This is a new field of studies: comparative medium-term studies of these changes are needed.

4

Citizenship and nationality in history teaching in post-communist Romania

Mirela-Luminiţa Murgescu and Cătălina Mihalache

Presenting a videogame on World War II, a columnist in the Romanian journal *Level* states candidly: 'While the alternative history textbooks shall remain with those who have written them, we will jump directly into the core of history, on the battlefield' (CronoX, 2005, 20). More thrilling and funnier than reality, the videogame allows direct action and quick decisions, for better or worse. In this vision of the world, textbooks can be seen as a rudimentary mediator, unable to provide an interactive interface in teaching history. Are videogames really competition for textbooks? Are they an alternative way of acquiring historical knowledge and of shaping behaviour, or just a passing fashion? Even if this were so, we have to consider them seriously, because they influence the way young people respond to traditional institutionalised education. And for an increasing segment of the population, modern media has become a significant means of constructing social (historical) memory and of shaping identities and patterns of behaviour.

In recent years, increasing numbers of educational researchers have examined history education as a means by which national identities are constructed and re-constructed. The programmes and publications of the Centre for Democracy and Reconciliation in Southeast Europe have outlined the specifics of the recent evolution of history education in the region. Volumes such as *Teaching the History of Southeastern Europe* (Kulouri, 2001) and Clio in the Balkans (Koulouri, 2002) provide an appraisal of history education throughout the region, and of its special connection with the construction of identities and of attitudes towards the Other.

> Most of the textbooks and history teaching in Southeastern Europe, as elsewhere, have been developed as part of the enterprise of creating nation-states. Since the nation represents such an important focus on identity in our region, and indeed in most of today's world, it would be both undesirable and unrealistic to try to deprive it of its place as the centre of the history curriculum. There is however a need, explored and illustrated by the articles in this Report, to combat stereotyping, which is the result of omitting less admirable episodes in one's own past and stressing those in the past of others, while omitting their achievements. There is certainly a need to give greater prominence to cultural history, which tends to be less divisive. Finally, there is no reason that history of nation-states should not be balanced by the teaching of histories focused on other potential focuses of identity as, for instance, local or regional. Even more radically, one might envisage a history of such institutions and concepts as citizenship, the rule of law, liberty and democracy, which would no longer be geographically focused but would bring together communities of differing time and place which remain however part of one intelligible 'story'. (Carras 2002, p13-14)

Both studies and practical experience show that the relationship between teaching citizenship and national affiliations is more difficult, and sometimes even painful, in states and societies where more national groups coexist, forming majorities and minorities.

> The Balkan experience does not leave much room for optimistic answers. Although the *topoi* of national imagination differ from one country to the next ... many structural components of the national narratives are the same. The worship of memory, but also the oblivion of painful events, the exaltation as well as the victimisation of nation, the particular projection of the past onto the mirrors of the

present and the future are features common in the most Balkan countries. ... Contemporary conflicts are projected into the past to appear as constant and unchanging throughout history. Thus they are perceived as inevitable, 'endemic' and therefore meant to re-surface *ad infinitum*. (Koulouri, 2002, p25-26)

(See also Papoulia-Tzelepi and Spinthourakis, Chapter 5 in this volume.)

Scholars and educators try to balance national identity with civic values. In this context, the first part of this chapter tries to provide a brief survey of the evolution of history teaching in post-communist Romania; we will outline some central issues, debates and options about the construction of social identities through history, and will also examine the way teachers and pupils respond to the changing discourses and curricula.

The second part of the chapter presents a case-study on the teaching of the events of 1918. This date is not random: it was a crucial year in Romanian history, when all Romanian territories were united in the Romanian state. It was also the moment when genuine efforts were made to accommodate minorities, and which can thus be used to help educate civic values. It is interesting to investigate whether, and to what extent, the opportunity to educate civic values was seized on, or at least perceived.

History and educational priorities in Romania after 1989

Apart from the textbook debate of 1999, triggered by the publication of a high-school textbook which tried to de-sanctify the teaching of Romanian history, there were no large public debates in post-communist Romania about the goals and priorities of history education, or ways to adapt it to meet the needs of contemporary society (Murgescu, 2004a). New curricula and syllabi were elaborated by small groups of experts, and enforced by the Ministry of Education.

The curricula for secondary schools (in Romanian called *gimnaziu*, pupils between 10-11 and 14-15 years old) adopted in 1999 gives general goals for history teaching:

> To understand and represent time and space in history, to know and assess sources, to investigate and assess facts and historical processes, to understand and use adequately scientific language, to stimulate curiosity for the study of history and to foster positive attitudes towards oneself and towards the others. (*Curriculum naţional* V-VIII, 1999, p25)

The history curricula for high schools (in Romanian called *lycee*, pupils between 14-15 and 18-19 years old) moves towards more concrete values and attitudes:

> The critical appropriation of roles determined by the affiliation to various identities (race, ethnicity, confession, nation, social corps, sex, profession). (*Curriculum naţional*, IX-XII, 1999, p23)

Note first the ambiguity in the possible identities, eg 'race' or 'social corps'. In this framework, history seems doomed to a vague and blurred approach towards civic values. The controversy over choosing the right name for national history supports this idea. In the 1990s there was a small debate whether to study the *History of Romania* or the *History of the Romanians*. The Regulations of the Ministry of Education, followed by the Education Law of 1995, settled on the *History of the Romanians*. But this choice was not based on a real debate on the meaning and on the implications of the two approaches: if we take terminology seriously, the two titles imply two different approaches to constructing memory and identities. *History of Romania* had been used during the communist rule, while *History of the Romanians* had prevailed before World War II. The authors of a high school textbook published in 1992, including the inspector responsible for history in the Ministry of Education, argued their option for the *History of the Romanians*:

> The need for a transition to a new textbook of national history compels us to ask ourselves how it should be entitled: *History of Romania* or *History of the Romanians*? For the first choice are several examples from other European countries or from the world. The authors of this textbook prefer the second alternative, taking into consideration the fact that the Romanians live in two distinct states, Romania and the Republic of Moldova, and also outside the borders of these two states. (Manea, Pascu and Teodorescu, 1992, p8)

The authors avoid outlining the consequences of their choice. They only acknowledge that:

> Naturally, the evolution of the Romanian people is presented in close connection with the life of the inhabitants of Hungarian, German, Serb, Bulgarian, Turkish and Tartar, Ukrainian, Jewish, Armenian and other nationalities, with due respect for all of them. (Manea, Pascu and Teodorescu, 1992, p8)

Note that the Roma population is not mentioned, in spite of its significant number; this omission is characteristic for the mental automatisms of Romanian historians, who rarely consider ethnic groups which have not developed their own state. The text includes lessons about the situation of those Romanians living under foreign dominion during the Middle Ages and the modern period, but somehow neglects Romanians dispersed in the Balkans, and includes no lessons, and practically no information, about the Romanians in the Soviet Union and its successor states after World War II, or the Romanians who had emigrated to various countries during the communist rule.

Thus the selection of *History of the Romanians* did not imply a major change in the structuring of national history taught in schools. The change was less about the contents, and more about the symbolism of history education. It was a way to stress that Romanian national history belongs more to the ethnic Romanians than to members of other nationalities. In this context, history education is more national than civic. History education was conceived of as more to preserve the identity and national memory of the ethnic Romanians and less as an instrument to construct and strengthen the memory of a civic nation which would include minorities. Of course, the authors have tried to be politically correct in arguing their choice:

> The natives (*autohtonii*), who form the majority nation, live together with the aliens (*alogenii*), the national minorities known today, for centuries on a land which models their nature, determines their occupations, [and] conditions their history. It is a history of active co-habitation, but also of episodic confrontations; therefore a history

full of lessons for all those who consider that freedom and civilisation, democracy and prosperity in independence are basic options. (Manea, Pascu and Teodorescu, 1992, p7)

This phrasing suggests a hierarchical relation between the Romanians and the members of the other nationalities. From one perspective, this means that the exclusion is somehow softened. Yet the memory of the minorities remains inferior and somehow external to the narrative of national history.

While the *History of the Romanians* focuses on the history of the ethnic Romanians, the minorities preferred to approach their specific history separately, in the framework of a special discipline. The Education Law stipulates that, in the schools for national minorities, the sixth and seventh grade students will be taught *the history and traditions of minorities*. This subject was included at the request of the representatives of the minorities, to provide specific historical and cultural education for the members of the ethnic minorities. The goals of the subject were formulated in the curricula for the Hungarian minority:

To know and to use the terms specific for Hungarian history and civilisation; to know and use sources on the past and the present of the Hungarian community; to understand time and historical space in the context of Hungarian civilisation; to participate at activities of local interest, which should provide positive value to the relations between the Hungarian minority and the majority population. (*Curriculum naţional*, V-VIII, 1999, p64)

In fact, the goals are similar in each of the curricula for the history and civilisation of the minorities, aiming basically to foster the specific identity of each minority. Generally, the curricula have two parts: one on the general history of the particular national community and a second one on the history of this community in the Romanian territories. An exception is the curricula for the German minority, which focuses only on the history and civilisation of the Germans in Romania. While the concern to provide to young people basic information about their own ethnic group is certainly legitimate, this pattern also risks building up mental Bantustans and blocking inter-ethnic communication. We suggest a better solution would be for a common subject including information about the traditions and history of all the minorities, which should be taught not only in the schools for minorities, but also in those for the majority of the population; in such a common framework, there could be included an optional module with additional information about a specific minority ethnic group.

Simultaneously, Romanian involvement in joining the European Union has generated a trend to education for a European identity. Thus it is not by chance that the last issue of the journal *Studii şi articole de istorie* (published by the Romanian Society for Historical Sciences (*Societatea de Ştiinţe Istorice din România*), the largest organisation of history teachers in Romania) included two articles that focus on history didactics as a way to educate European citizenship.

> History, alone or in correlation with other disciplines, contributes considerably to the understanding of key concepts – cooperation and conflict, democracy and dictatorship, freedom and order, equality and diversity, rights and responsibilities, tolerance and intolerance, justice and law etc. – for the formation/development of democratic attitudes and values. (Vitanos, 2005, p177)

Such articles show that at least some history teachers are aware of the need to adapt the goals and methods of history education. This openness is also shown in those history teachers who participated in methodological projects and teacher-training programmes. But it is difficult to assess the extent of this openness, and what really happens in the practice of the education system. Attitudes about history education were often divided, and doubts have been increased by the reduction of teaching hours, so that in most grades and studies there is now only one hour per week for history (until the mid-1990s there had been an average of two hours a week). This reduction, reflecting how history has lost ground in competition with other disciplines and has a diminishing status, undermines attempts to modernise history education and to use it to form civic values and attitudes.

What has happened at the level of history textbooks?

In post-communist Romania, the renewal of history textbooks has passed through several stages (Murgescu, 2004b). After an abortive attempt to simply reintroduce a textbook from the pre-communist period, following minor revisions of the communist textbooks, there were two generations of new textbooks, one in 1992/1993 and one in the late 1990s. In the early 1990s there was only one textbook for each grade; after 1995 there was a shift towards alternative textbooks, authorised by the National Council for Textbook Approval (*Comisia Naţională pentru Aprobarea Manualelor*).

Social and political pressures on textbook authors and on the syllabi diminished after 1990, but did not disappear. Authors enjoyed more freedom, especially after the establishment of alternative textbooks. Although authors often complain about the national syllabi, these have been rather vague and left a large margin for the textbook author. The time/space constraints were more severe (the number of teaching hours and pages), and the drive to adjust historical discourse to meet public expectations was stepped up in order to conquer a larger share of the textbook market.

The textbook scandal of 1999 served as a warning for publishers and textbook authors that history education was ideologically sensitive and that it was wiser to comply to the prevailing narrative of national history. The scandal arose when a group of young historians from Cluj published a 12th-grade textbook in which they deconstructed several myths of Romanian history. Their book met a furious reaction from public opinion, the media, historians and politicians.

One of the main accusations against the textbook and its authors was that they included a lesson entitled *The 'invention' of the modern nation* (Mitu, 1999), based on Benedict Anderson's concept of *imagined community*; the critics also complained that traditionally celebrated historical figures (for example, the Dacian king Decebal, the Roman emperor Trajan, or the medieval princes Stephan the Great and Michael the Brave) were assigned only a few lines, which was perceived as vulgarising and trivial.

Although this textbook was revised in 2000, it was still prohibited from schools through an order of the Minister of Education in 2001. The scandal of 1999, and the prohibition of the textbook, showed how strong taboos about historical knowledge and especially the teaching of history in school persist in Romanian society.

Ethnicity, identity, citizenship and schoolbooks

Ethnicity is at the core of Romanian identity. It has a double function: it identifies the Romanians and it integrates them into European identity. The history of the Romanians is the history of the Romanian ethnicity, shaped by Latin origin and Christianity.

> The Romanians belong to European civilisation, first through their Latin origin and Christian faith. Like the Italians, French, Spaniards etc. they are the inheritors of the Roman Empire of two thousand years ago. But, while all other Latin people live in Western and Southern Europe, are grouped and neighbour one another, only the Romanians are relatively isolated and placed between Slavs and Hungarians. Therefore, many historians and linguists have considered the Romanian a 'miracle' or an 'enigma', not necessarily regarding the way they emerged, but because they have survived and kept their Romanic characteristics in the midst of 'Slav sea and in the way of waves of migrants and invaders'. (Cârțănă *et al,* 2000, p3).

Textbooks insist on emphasising the difference between the Romanians and their neighbours, and ethnicity is the crucial element.

> At the same time, the Romanians differentiated from their neighbours. They looked both to the East and to the West, because they spoke a Latin language and claimed their descent from the Romans. Regarding their development, in the fifteenth to eighteenth centuries the Romanians distanced themselves fundamentally from the Southern Slavs and from the Greeks. (Cârțănă *et al,* 2000, p3)

Latin ethnicity was perceived as paramount in the affiliation as a major cultural and linguistic component of Western Europe, and thus for claiming the European-ness of the Romanians. This pattern has been strengthened by the current process of European integration. History textbooks try to link Latin ethnicity to Romania's joining the European Union.

Europe is not only a geographical space, Europe marks an affiliation. Being in Europe means for our people to be together with others in the aspiration for progress and civilisation. Being ethnically (through their Latin origin) and religiously (through their Christian faith) in Europe, the Romanians had and still have to fight with themselves and with various external forces in order to really be in the community of democratic and prosperous nations and states. (Bozgan *et al,* 1999, p3)

Beyond textbooks

Historians and education scholars know that the content of textbooks is only part of the picture, and that the reactions of teachers and pupils are more important in determining the effectiveness of history education. We have therefore also tried to examine what might be called the consumer perspective on history education. We started from the following statement by a teacher:

... I recall the theatrical reaction of one of my fellow female colleagues, who [referring to the] controversial debates about the newly published alternative optional history textbooks, stated that the new authors have 'murdered the beloved Medieval princes and the national history so dear to our students'. (*We and our neighbours*, 2004, p17)

In order to check the representativeness of such an opinion, we investigated several high schools from Bucharest, Jassy and Caracal. We created a questionnaire which included tick-box and open-ended responses. For logistical reasons we did not seek a representative national sample, but used colleagues to distribute the questionnaire to pupils and students. We received answers from 126 pupils and 26 graduate students and teachers.

The questionnaire asked respondents to define *History of Romania* and *History of the Romanians*. Neither pupils nor teachers had a clear opinion on the difference between the two concepts or approaches. For many respondents, *History of Romania* meant only the history of the modern Romanian state: a sixteen year old female answered that *History of Romania* refers 'strictly to Romania as a state and to the way it was formed'. Only one of the 152 answers stated that *History of Romania* is 'the history and evolution of the people who lived in this space throughout time' (fifteen years old, male). For most respondents, *History of the Romanians* refers to 'the struggle of the Romanians for independence, the things they had to confront and for which they fought a long time' (nineteen years old, female).

Another question asked about the role of history education. Although the question was open and formulated very generally, the answers we received focused on national history. In a Romantic pattern, history was perceived as 'the first book of the nation', and the 'evocation of facts from the past of the Romanians which are worthy to be remembered by our contemporaries'. History is ethnically appropriated: it is 'our' history, the history of our people, and also strongly event-focused, emphasising the importance of wars and rulers.

Both pupils and teachers consider that history is important in forming the Romanian identity. History is 'very important because it justifies our national identity'. 'It is very good to know your genealogy. You must know where from you have your roots. You are more confident when you know that there can be written a history of your people' (nineteen years old, female). 'We enjoy a sentiment of pride and equilibrium in relationship with other nations because our people has moments of pride in its history and we have with what to eulogise towards others' (nineteen years old female). 'History teaches us not to forget that we are Romanians and shows to us the price paid by our ancestors in order that we have today our own country and language' (thirty year old teacher, male).

All other goals are secondary to national education. Nevertheless, there are opinions that history should also help 'to develop knowledge of general culture and provide information useful for the future'. History even 'teaches us to avoid mistakes made in the past and to have positive attitudes towards those who are not like us' (eighteen year old, female), but such opinions were few among the answers.

Our survey confirms the hypothesis that most pupils and teachers share an ethno-centric vision of history, which is supported by historians and textbooks. History education continues to be perceived as nation-building. Sensitive issues like the relationship between ethnic and civic nation have not really been debated by the professional historians in Romania, and have even less penetrated into school education. For most teachers and pupils, the nation-state is the normal way to structure the world, and each (ethnic) nation is entitled to its own nation-state.

When asked about the Romanians living in other states and the minorities living in the Romanian state, both pupils and teachers answer instinctively and often in random manner. This lack of rigour can be seen in the answers to an item about Antim Ivireanul, a clergyman who contributed significantly to Romanian culture around 1700; asked whether his name indicates that he was ethnically not Romanian (*Ivireanul* comes from *Iviria*, in present-day Georgia, Caucasus), a large number of the respondents (especially in Moldavia) answer negatively – that is, that he was Romanian in origin.

Both textbooks and the perceptions of teachers and pupils highlight concerns about the effectiveness of attempts to modernise history education in Romania. Although some stereotypes have been eliminated from textbooks, prejudices persist; in spite of progress in disseminating civic values, the mental framework of history education still favours ethnic nationalism.

A case study: teaching 1918 in Romania

We have chosen the year 1918 for a case study of the relationship between nationality and citizenship in history teaching in Romania. As we have said above, the choice of year was not random. In 1918, at the end of World War I, Bessarabia, Bukovina and Transylvania successively united with the Romanian state, a process which was internationally sealed by the peace treaties of Paris in 1919-1920. Thus, large numbers of Romanians who had enjoyed only minority status in Russia and Austro-Hungary became part of the majority nation, while Hungarians, Germans and Russians were relegated to minority status. Statements were made during this political process that the attempt to build a nation-state would be fair to minorities. This year can thus be used to educate about civic values for both the majority and for minorities. It can be also used to strengthen national identity and to isolate each ethnic group in its own version of history.

An initial observation: while, for most Europeans, 1918 means the end of World War I, Romanians are taught less to remember the war and more to be proud of accomplishing national unity. In Romanian history, 1918 is presented as the realisation of a century-long dream of the Romanians: Greater Romania, fulfilled through the inclusion of the whole (or most) of the Romanian ethnic peoples in the same state. The hardships and sacrifices of the war are overshadowed by the triumph of the Great Union.

While the historical sources document complex and various attitudes of people living the events, history education has severely simplified facts and evidence, in order to include the events of 1918 in a teleological narrative, culminating with the achievement of the unitary nation-state. This grand narrative is extremely influential and, in 1990, 1st December was chosen as the national holiday for post-communist Romania, recalling the day in 1918 when a national assembly, convened in Alba Iulia, decided on the unification of Transylvania with Romania.

Before discussing current textbooks, we should note that, to a large extent, the approach towards 1918 was inherited from the period before 1989. Surveying the way these events were studied during late communism, during the first transitional years in the early 1990s and in more recent years, can help us not only better understand this particular issue, but also assess the degree of change in history education in post-communist Romania. Over the last fifteen years, school curricula, authors, editors, teachers and students have all endured an official process of reforming, alongside other countless and uncontrolled changes. All are somehow reflected in textbooks, which also shelter various resistance to change. These elements of inertia are a support to identity and could be seen as powerful locations of national memory, challenging the politics of the moment.

Before exploring the groups of schoolbooks for these three periods, we should notice some common structures. Romanian history is taught in three sequences, at the end of each stage of schooling: the principle is to increase information at each level, and also to add to the complexity of historical analysis – but in the latter respect, much is still in the stage of *pious desiderata*. Thus Romania in 1918 is now taught to pupils in the fourth, eighth and twelfth grades. In the 1980s, Romanian history was taught over five years (now only three years) and the lessons on 1918 were in the fourth, ninth, and twelfth grades: this is only a minor change, and the structure of the narrative is the same as it was in the 1980s.

The story is told in two separate lessons. The first is about Romanian participation in World War I (from 1916 to 1918), the second focuses on the completion of Romanian national unification, almost exclusively in 1918. This split in the narration is for political, rather than chronological reasons (the chronology is ambiguous and incomplete). National unity is presented as the happy ending of a long history of injustice and sacrifices, which include those endured in the latest war. The division and the selection of events serves to depict the unification process as a peaceful and democratic manifestation of the self-determination of the Romanian nation, according to the international political rules of the post-war times.

Other continuities can be noticed at the level of the textbook. While the communist national history textbooks for gymnasium (*gimnaziu*) and high schools (*licee*) remained in use, with only minor changes, until 1992/1993, in the elementary schools the history textbook for the fourth grade (by Dumitru Almas) was republished with only minor changes until 1995.

Learning about 1918 in 1989

Opening a fourth grade history textbook published before 1989, one is first struck by the archaic and emotional language of the presentation. The pictures are poor reproductions, rigidly disposed across the text. The chapter '*The making of the Romanian united national state*' is almost entirely placed at the end of 1918. The political requirement to omit past difficulties with Russia led to a complete silence on Bessarabia. The unification process that is described focuses on Transylvania, and clearly follows the ideological command of the period: the textbook insists that there was goodwill from the Hungarians and the Germans living in this province, who agreed with what Romanians did. At the same time, 'they were promised to have equal rights with the Romanians' (Almaş, 1985, p129). This is all that is said about the others. The story immediately returns to the happiness of the Romanians, suggesting that from this moment on, being *equal to* is the only meaning of *to be* Romanian.

In the ninth grade texts, more details were added under the same heading. Giving detail was considered to guarantee precision, and this was equated with science, objectivity, truth and a superior expression of patriotism. Only in the high school did the Ministry allowed a few mentions of the unification of Bessarabia and Bukovina with the Romanian state. Claiming that the most important political decisions were made by 'the representations of the population' living in these territories (Hurezeanu *et al*, 1988, p203, 207), the textbook leaves curious pupils to guess that this might not always refer to Romanians. Opposition is never mentioned: on the contrary, the already established Others (the Hungarians and the Germans from Transylvania) were described as being soon 'well fitted into the united Romanian state' (Hurezeanu *et al*, 1988, p207), so it was considered unnecessary to refer to them again.

What past could be brought by the revolution?

In December 1989 the regime was smashed, the dictator killed and the Ministry of Education totally confused. Liberating textbooks from communism was a very unexpected job for school authorities and historians. For the next two years, truth was to be found rather personally, each teacher concerned to avoid a certain vocabulary, exploring pre-communist memoirs and historical works that were previously banished. Exclusion of material was much easier, as it had been during communism. Most of the textbooks of 1980s (especially for studying world history) were still used in classrooms, with minimal omissions.

There was a short-lived attempt in the high schools (*lycees*) to teach Romanian history based on a textbook originally published in 1944, with Petre Panaitescu credited as author, and republished in identical form in 1990. Significantly for the communist appropriation of pre-communist nationalism, the old book was very similar to the 1980s version in the way it treated the events of 1918. The nationalist element was even more aggressive in Panaitescu's textbook: the Romanians were encouraged to remember how they had fought and defeated the Hungarians. Only the Germans (Saxons) from Transylvania were praised, for accepting unification (Panaitescu, 1990, p323). The author insisted that in Bessarabia the Romanians decided all, and did not even name any other ethnic minorites (Panaitescu, 1990, p322). Ignoring minorities, or simply those who were different, was common.

Panaitescu's text had been published during World War II, so attempt to instil this fighting spirit in youngsters might be considered an ideological part of the war effort. But as political and ethnic conflicts brought Romania close to civil war in 1990, some consideration must be given to the choice to teach history of that sort half a century after the events. The same nationalist approach towards 1918 also governed the choice of December 1st as a national holiday in post-communist Romania.

The first revised textbooks of national history started to be published in 1991 to 1992, though still only one textbook for each grade. The amount of information included for high schools was very greatly augmented, turning textbooks into huge depositories of facts. At the same time, Romanian history became an important subject for examination in high school graduation, and for admission to university. Textbooks in these years offer quantities of military data about unification: for example, pupils in the eighth grade were taught how Russians and Ukrainians disturbed Romania's eastern and northern provinces and how Hungarians were aggressive towards Romanians in Transylvania (Cristescu *et al*, 1993, p98-100). The obvious conclusion to be drawn was that we had been attacked and we had to legitimately defend our territories in order to create Greater

Romania. Pupils were expected to be proud of this successful fighting with neighbours, and to prepare themselves to mourn the loss of land in the future in 1940.

The twelfth-grade textbook had the goal not of informing, but of presenting a detailed history. On the events in Bessarabia, the textbook mentions that 'representatives of all nationalities' in the province were called on to decide its future, but the authors do not bother to specify who these nationalities were (Manea and Teodorescu, 1994, 225). When referring to Bukovina, the authors suggest a multiple ethnic profile by identifying groups who favoured Romanian unification (Poles, Germans and Ruthenians). The context was arranged to show again that, while the Romanians were indeed in the majority in voting for unification, they were not an absolute majority of the inhabitants. The deputies representing the Jewish population are not remembered, because they did not vote for Greater Romania. The happy-ending approach of accepting and recognising the Romanian will in Bukovina is simply a way of closing the subject (Manea and Teodorescu, 1994, p226).

The hostile attitude of the Hungarian population towards Transylvania was described with insistence. It was stated in these texts that, while only a part of the population accepted the unification, this was the democratic part. Democracy is here being understood as pro-Romanian action, in the same way that the German and Jewish Congresses which recognised the unification had been recognised. But the democratic way was not the only process leading to political victory. The conclusion of these events was not reconciliation – as we might have expected – but was brought about by the Romanian army that conquered Budapest in August 1919 (Manea and Teodorescu, 1994, p227-230).

But this level of detailing also had adverse implications. The textbooks reproduced in full the assembly of Alba Iulia resolution that decided Transylvania's union with Romania, but there were also clear promises formulated for minorities. The copious level of detail about the joyous consequences of the Great Unification mean that the events slowly fade from the historical narrative as an outcome of partly remembering the others and their different options. Silences and false agreements gradually turned into hostile remembrance and stories of unfinished wars.

Teaching 1918 now

The textbooks of 1992 and 1993 were removed as systems of alternative textbooks developed in agreement with the World Bank and in the context of curricula changes that left only three years for studying *the history of the Romanians*. From 1995, the Ministry has gradually allowed schools and teachers to choose one of several officially approved alternatives. For the first time since the end of the communist regime, challenge to the truths and a multiplicity of opinions were officially promoted. But this soon became of a competition between publishing houses rather than a public stage for the views of historians who had been silenced for a long time.

The fourth grade had three approved textbooks. One mentions only the Romanians in describing what happened in 1918. Their decisions and their state were considered to be so important that even the war is renamed as the 'war for the re-completion of the nation', exaggerating the old formula used in the 1920s for the participation of the Romanian kingdom in World War I (Grigore *et al,* 2000, p71).

Another device is one of speaking only about the Romanians, but then finally adding a phrase such as that, through unification, 'the minorities were granted the conditions in which they could affirm their national identities' (Burlec *et al*, 1997, p83).

The third textbook includes the names of some of the nationalities in Transylvania (Saxons, Hungarians and Szeklers), but only to add how they saluted 'our' unification as an 'act of justice for the Romanians' and a promise for a peaceful future (Ochescu and Oane, 2001, p77). This approach replaces omission with a biased – and rather naïve – selection of information that is made to support an optimistic and simplistic Romanian national identity.

In the eighth grade, three textbooks were also approved , and the space devoted to the lessons of 1918 are considerably increased. In one of these the Romanians are, again, the only ethnic element involved in the processes of building Greater Romania (Lazăr and Lupu, 2001, p139-141). Another notes the presence of dangerous Ukrainian nationalists in Bukovina, and that unification of the province with Romania was also voted for by Poles, Germans and (good) Ukrainians. On the Transylvania situation, it is suddenly stated that 'Hungary refused to recognise the unification' (Vulpe *et al*, 2000, p104) – but immediately before reading this, one is assured of the acceptances declared by 'the minorities from the province, Saxons, Swabians, Jews and a part of the Hungarians' (Vulpe *et al*, 2000, p104). There is also progress. One assignment is to 'explain the attitude of the national minorities from Transylvania toward the act of the unification with Romania' (Vulpe *et al*, 2000, p105), and this may encourage pupils to turn the page and search for the promises made by the Romanians on December 1st 1918. The authors also admit that in Greater Romania these promises were only partially fulfilled, but suggest that the outcome was in any case better than previous conditions for Romanians in Habsburg-ruled Transylvania (Vulpe *et al*, 2000, p106).

The last of the three eighth-grade history texts simply mentions some 'other inhabitants' agreeing with the Romanians in Bukovina (Oane and Ochescu, 2001, 120). The same insensitive label can also be found in a twelfth-grade textbook, (Brezeanu *et al*, 2000, p156), while others only mention Romanians (Bozgan *et al*, 1999, p89).

One of the texts for the twelfth grade goes so far as to tell of those who refused unification with Romania, even of those like the Romanian Aurel Onciul, who preferred a Ukrainian authority in Bukovina (Dumitrescu *et al*, 1999, p124). The authors don't manage to develop this identity paradox to suggest that political pluralism was (and is) legitimate and that, even in such glorious days, several different political options had been expressed. Opposition is generally blamed as being an historical accident, usually concerning foreigners: 'Ukrainian ultra-nationalist organisations and some hostile Hungarians, who maintained these feelings even after unification' (Scurtu *et al*, 2000, p154, 156). Unanimity is required about our past and this could be an echo of the language of the late communist period, that was so obsessed by Romanian unity, oneness and uniformity. Unification is characterised as a 'unanimous decision' (Cârţână *et al*, 2000, p118) or at least as the decision of a large majority, even if events prove this to be false. For example, a textbook of 1999 describes the demographic situation in Bukovina in 1918 as 'Romanians and minority people' (Scurtu *et al*, 1999, p99), although the Romanians were never the absolute majority in the province as a whole.

The same pattern of eliminating mention of minorities is true for Bessarabia. The texts never fail to recall the historical arguments of the Romanian claim on Bessarabia in 1918, but always avoid discussing either that this issue was muted in the first war years (when Romania was allied with Russia) or the concrete demographic situation in this province

We must now refer to the text which provoked a large public controversy in late 1999, and which almost compromised the idea of an alternative historical discourse in post-communist Romania. The scandalous exploitation of rigid expressions of patriotism and habits of teaching is now history (Murgescu, 2004a, p109-167), but in 2001 it produced the first example of the Ministry of Education suppressing a previously approved textbook – moreover, a text that had been 'softened' and 'improved' for its second edition in 2000. This textbook was seen, especially in its first edition, as anti-nationalist, and it was celebrated as a fine expression of de-constructionism in historical (cultural) studies. This iconoclastic approach did not include a narrative on 1918, so this part did not need significant revision for its second edition. The narrative is populated by the same Romanian majorities, the usual confusion between territories and the people living in them, some bad Ukrainians, and a list of ethnic names who approved unification (Mitu, 1999, p84-85; Mitu, 2000, p92-93). This textbook nevertheless offers clues for understanding a favourite telling of the history of Romania.

One phrase about the unification of 1918 was deleted in the second edition: this concerned the presence of the Romanian army in the new united territories. The first edition stated that the Romanian political leaders of the moment 'insisted on demonstrating that Unification was not the result of military conquest, but was the option of the populations living in the respective zones' (Mitu, 1999, p84). In 1999. people paid little attention to this assertion. In the next edition, the authors excluded the sentence, following a long tradition of exercising self-censorship, in order to counter new accusations of not being good Romanian citizens, who must love their past and expose it in a loveable manner. Erasure is the recognition of what is better lost in silence: the difference, the others, the losers and their complaining (Ferro, 1984). It is characteristic of a historical discourse still trapped by the loyalties of the nineteenth century and by the long instilled interdictions of the communist age.

It is not only ethnic or political differences that are still omitted or minimised in textbooks, but also confessional differences. For example, the Catholics from Transylvania are never mentioned as a special entity, although they included most of the Romanian intellectuals and political leaders in the area. Violence against Jews in the interwar period is also overlooked. In fact, the joy of unification was accompanied by the permanent suspicion of the Romanians from the *Old Kingdom* of all the inhabitants of the new provinces. But these fears have no place in telling the glorious story of national unity, in spite of the formal requirement of the curriculum to discuss the issue of unity and diversity in Greater Romania (*Curriculum national*, 1999, IX-XII, p33).

If we want to condense all the pages of the textbooks quoted into an single representation of Romania in 1918, we should look for images. Most textbooks include the same pictures of the participants at the Great National Assembly held in Alba Iulia, on December 1st 1918, which proclaimed the unification of Transylvania with Romania. The large number of participants is the main subject, and social diversity – easy recognisable through clothing (priests, officers, peasants and few city people) – adds to the impression of multitude and unanimity. The pervasive idea is that all the participants were Romanians and they all agreed to the unification. The photos are not explained, so they cannot be contradicted. Images are entirely subordinated to the text, inducing a mass effect and the symbolical dissolution of the leaders into the timeless body of the nation.

In the last decade there were serious efforts to diminish the potential of history education to foster conflict. This was politically meaningful and was also generous but, while societies continue to prefer to teach only their own version of history in schools, it is inconceivable that the nationalistic pattern will be replaced by a civic and more democratic paradigm. Unfortunately, there will always be someone who will try to persuade us all that the enemy is at the gates.

5

History teaching and the educated citizen: the case of history teaching in the Greek gymnasium

Panayota Papoulia-Tzelepi and
Julia A Spinthourakis

The significance of History teaching

Knowledge of history is the precondition of political intelligence. Without history, a society shares no common memory of where it has been, what its core values are, or what decisions of the past account for present circumstances. Without history, we cannot undertake any sensible inquiry into the political, social, or moral issues in society. And without historical knowledge and inquiry, we cannot achieve the informed, discriminating citizenship essential to effective participation in the democratic processes of governance and the fulfilment for all our citizens of the nation's democratic ideals. (National Centre for History in Schools, National Standards in History 1996 p1)

At least two questions arise from this statement, since we live in the era of globalisation, where the pace of change is great and the future monopolises the attention and concerns of millions. The first is: is there any place for history? The second: does the statement above have any relevance in our time? It seems that societies and nations reply positively to both questions: discussions and debates, books, curricula, conferences and training attest to people's preoccupation with history teaching in school (e.g. Sebba, 1997; Stearns *et al*, 2000; Husbands, 1992, 1996). Nevertheless this concern for history teaching is not unqualified. After painful inquiry and judgement, modern societies would like to have the ability to determine what part of history is relevant to current problems when one is accessing a situation, forming an opinion or taking an active position on an issue. In exploring these matters, students will soon discover that history is filled with the high costs of decisions reached on the basis of false analogies from the past, as well as the costs of actions taken with little or no understanding of the important lessons of the past.

Others see history teaching and learning as contributing to the development of an individual identity, as historical memory is the key to self-identity, to seeing one's place in time and one's connectedness to the ancient chain of humanity (Southgate, 2000; Furay and Salevouris, 2000). This provides a sense of shared community on which one's personal development and responsible citizenship depend.

Properly engaged, history teaching and learning provide students with opportunities to develop an awareness and understanding of the world and the wealth of different cultures, enriching experience and allowing for better understanding of themselves and their society.

In view of this, what should be the goals of history teaching and learning in the new millennium? *National Standards for History* (1996) in the United States defines the goals as follows:

- Historical thinking skills that enable students to evaluate evidence, develop comparative and causal analyses, interpret the historical record, and construct sound historical arguments and perspectives on which informed decisions in contemporary life can be based.

- Historical understanding that defines what students know about the history of their nation and of the world. These

> understandings are drawn from the record of human aspirations, strivings, accomplishments, and failures in at least five spheres of human activity: the social, political, scientific/technological, economic, and cultural (philosophical/religious/aesthetic). They also provide students with the historical perspectives required to analyse contemporary issues and problems confronting citizens today. (National Centre for History in Schools (USA), *Definition of Standards* 1996, p1)

In the 19th century, and continuing throughout the greater part of the 20th century, history teaching almost exclusively focused on political history. Jenkins (1996) suggests that the move towards a broader perspective came from a growing awareness that such an approach did not do justice to the wealth and breadth of past human experience, and that it also limited the educative power of history teaching, along with advances in scientific historical thinking.

This new and broader perspective integrates spheres of activity, including the social, political, scientific/technological, economic and cultural, showing how each is tightly interwoven with the other. Integrating these five spheres accomplishes the twin goals of historical thinking and historical understanding. At the same time, new curricula and teaching approaches in history move away from historical knowledge as a passive absorption of facts, dates, names and places (Peck, 2005). These approaches conceptualise history learning and teaching as a process of reasoning based on evidence from the past, grounded in the careful gathering of factual information. However the process does not stop here.

According to the authors of the *National Standards for History,*

> ... real historical understanding requires students to think through cause-and-effect relationships, to reach sound historical interpretations, and to conduct historical inquires and research leading to the knowledge on which informed decisions in contemporary life can be based. These thinking skills are the processes of active learning. (National Standards for History, Developing Standards in History for Students 1996, p1)

Towards this end, it appears that, to acquire the capacity to analyse and make judgments, students must develop competences in five types of historical thinking:

1) chronological thinking

2) historical comprehension

3) historical analysis and interpretation

4) historical research

5) historical issues analysis

(*ibid* p2)

These skills, though presented in five separate categories, are related and mutually supportive. In conducting historical research or creating an historical argument of their own, for example, students must be able to draw upon skills in all five categories. Beyond the skills of conducting their research, students must be able to comprehend historical documents and records, analyse their relevance, develop interpretations of the document(s) they select, and demonstrate a sound grasp of their meaning (Stearns, Seixas and Wineburg, 2000).

What to teach? The problem of content

One of the biggest controversies in teaching history in schools is what to include. Will it be the ethnocentric master narrative, in which one's own people is conceptualised as brave, high-minded, and superior to others? Unfortunately, this is the content of history teaching in most cases. Rüsen (2004; see also Chapter 2 in this volume) sees this as a consequence of the needs for identity formation. He argues succinctly that

Identity has always been an issue of values. A convincing concept of identity furnished the people with self-esteem. Since identity has always been grounded on a difference from the otherness of the others, the positive evaluation of oneself logically leads to a negative view on the otherness of the others. And this is the fundamental problem of ethnocentrism – the deeply rooted and universally spread mode of filling the difference between self and others with positive and negative values. Since the others follow the same logic of one's own people, there is a mutual devaluation in intercultural relationships. By this logic of identity-formation a fundamental and universal clash of civilisations results. The history of all civilisations is full of this asymmetrical evaluation in the process of identity-formation. The people ascribe positive values to themselves and define the 'otherness' of the others by deviations or even contradictions to these values. (Rüsen, 2004, p32)

But a completely opposite case may be argued: today's students, more than ever before, need to understand comprehensively the history of the world and of the many cultures and civilisations which have developed ideas, institutions and ways of life different from the student's own. A balanced and inclusive world history may give students an appreciation of the world's many cultures and of their shared humanity and common problems. Students may develop the habit of seeing through the eyes of others, and of coming to realise that by studying others they can also better understand themselves.

Historical understanding based on comparative studies in world history does not require either approval or forgiveness for the tragedies – of one's own society or of others' – nor does it negate the importance of critically examining alternative value systems and how they support or deny basic human rights and aspirations. As the National Centre for History in Schools (1996) suggests, an understanding of the history of the world's many cultures can contribute to fostering the mutual patience, respect and civic courage required in increasingly pluralistic societies and an increasingly interdependent world.

Recommendations of the Council of Europe

The Council of Europe (COE) project *Learning and teaching about the history of Europe in the 20th century* adopted an interdisciplinary and pan-European stance, which stressed the importance of social, scientific, cultural and oral history (COE, 1999, 2000a, 2000b). The project encouraged teaching history using a range of sources, such as new technologies, cinema, women's history, archives and museums, and developed the concept of remembrance as vital to the prevention of crimes against humanity.

Teaching 20th Century European History (COE, 2000b) is a comprehensive handbook on teaching 20th century history, laying the groundwork for approaching themes and topics from a European perspective and for multi-perspectivity, encouraging students to investigate the experience of those holding opposing and unpopular viewpoints. It provides a methodology for developing the skills of research and assessment in handling historical sources, particularly media and new technologies. It promotes the understanding of others through role-play and the teaching of sensitive and controversial issues.

A direct result of the project was Recommendation No R (2001) 15 of the Committee of Ministers, the first text adopted at a pan-European level to set out clear methodological principles on the objectives of history teaching in a democratic and pluralist Europe. This covers the aims of history teaching, the European dimension, the content of the syllabus, learning methods, teacher training and information and communication technologies. It also addresses the misuse of history, condemning this and giving examples of the abuse of the historical record and interpretations of history based upon an us/them dichotomy: both are incompatible with the values of the Council of Europe.

In this framework of international trends and changes in history teaching we now present the situation in Greece. Our focus outlines how the new curriculum and new textbooks are expected to respond to these challenges for history teaching for the citizens of the 21st century. Parallel to this, we also present background on the current educational parameters of the system and what must be taught in the lower secondary school in history. Finally, we provide examples of the role that fluctuating ethnic and nationalist ideological tides play in the teaching of history in Greece, with specific reference to the challenges in teaching history related to the Turks and the Ottoman Empire, the role of the Greek Orthodox Church in the formation of the Greek national identity and the relationship of the Greek Civil War with the state's stance towards the Soviet Union.

Teaching history of the Greek Gymnasium (13-15 years old)

The system and curricular reform

All levels of schooling in Greece are tuition free, and books are also distributed, free of charge, to students and teachers. The system has three tiers: a six-year elementary phase, a six-year secondary phase and higher education. The secondary tier is divided into Gymnasium (three years) and Lyceum (three years): the former phase is compulsory.

Educational policy reforms in the last few years have centred on reversing longstanding centralisation, but the system remains largely centralised. A rather detailed curriculum framework is expected to be uniformly followed across the entire country. Up to recently, the curriculum has been implemented through a series of grade-specific textbooks and teachers' guidebooks, in which virtually everything was prescribed in detail. In many respects this has been an example of a higher-end closed curriculum paradigm (OECD, 1994, 191-92; OECD, 1998). Greek state educational policy reforms in the late 1990s and early 2000s focused on moving away from this towards a more open and innovative expression of the curriculum (Georgiadis, 2005). Our focus in this chapter will be on the new curriculum for history in the Gymnasium, grades 1, 2 and 3, for the age range of 13 to 15 years old.

History curriculum for the Greek Gymnasium

The main thrust of the new curriculum is its cross-thematic nature (*diathematiko*), offering a cross between an interdisciplinary and concept-based curriculum (Alahiotis and Karatzia-Stavlioti, 2006). Although the new curriculum for compulsory education (6 to 15 years old) maintains the traditional school subjects in separate disciplines, it follows a holistic approach to content, which stresses cross-disciplinary connections and relationships rather than divisions between academic disciplines. It emphasises the processes through which academic knowledge has been produced and used, and the values and attitudes associated with academic knowledge, thought and work in an academic way (Alahiotis, 2004). It is hoped that this will help students to understand the world they live in.

Using the project method during the school year and at the end of each semester (Frey, 1994), students are expected to work in each subject on topics related to the content: these deepen their understanding and develop their cognitive and social skills and attitudes, all of which are perceived as necessary for active involvement in future life.

The goals, content, teaching approaches and the evaluation of the Greek curriculum in history teaching are published as part of the official curriculum document in the National Gazette, FEK B, 303/ 13-03-03, by Presidential Decree, which has the power of national law (Greek Ministry of Education and Religious Affairs, 2003). This document is used in this chapter, either verbatim or paraphrasing and summarising its content.

The aims

The Greek national curriculum (Greek Ministry of Education and Religious Affairs, 2003) gives the aim of teaching history as the development of historical thinking and historical conscience. Historical thinking concerns understanding historical facts by examining causes and effects, and historical conscience the understanding of human behaviour in concrete situations, developing responsible values and attitudes that will shape students' behaviour. The students realise through the study of history how the contemporary world is a continuation of the past and directly connected with their lives. These aims relate to the general aim of education, the preparation of responsible citizens.

In secondary education, specific goals in the study of history are to become familiar with historical terminology, critical choice and use of historical sources and to become aware that understanding a particular time or society entails studying political, economic, cultural and religious aspects. Students should also develop tolerance and respect for difference, and an understanding of how Greek civilisation relates to others and the contribution of the Greeks to the world.

84

The content

The problem of what to teach in history is particularly difficult in the case of Greece, where more than 3,500 years of history must be condensed into two hours a week over the three years of the Gymnasium. The ambitious curriculum aims at also covering some European history and a little world history in the same period. Some of this content, but at a lower level of complexity, is also covered in the upper elementary school (with 10 to 12 years olds).

The history subject agenda for these three years is consequently quite full:

■ First year: Prehistory, the Copper Age in the Aegean, Cycladic, Minoan and Mycenaean Civilisations, the Homeric Age, the Greek colonies in the Mediterranean, the Classical years, Alexander the Great, Hellenistic times, and the Romans

■ Second year: Byzantine civilisation, the Crusades, the Turks and the fall of the Byzantine Empire, Medieval Europe, Europe from 15th-18th century, the Greeks under Venetian Control and the Greeks under Turkish occupation

■ Third year: the Enlightenment, American and French Revolutions, the Greek Revolution and the Modern Greek state, the Industrial Revolution, Science, Literature and Technology in Europe and Greece during the 19th century, the First World War, the Russian Revolution, the Asia Minor Greek catastrophe, the Second World War, the Cold War, Greece after the war, and intellectual, scientific and artistic developments in the 20th century

In parallel to this linear study, a recent innovation means that students also study local history for ten hours each year (Alahiotis, 2004). Activities are suggested for all sections, such as discussions, comparisons, using maps, diagrams and artefacts, and studying the influence of financial, technological, artistic and communication in historical events such as the Olympiads.

Finally, collaborative group-oriented project work is suggested, covering a wide range of topics and methods of implementation.

Examples of these are the measurement of time from antiquity to the present, law-making in the Byzantine period, technology in wartime, the major modern inventions and their implications, the Enlightenment, dwellings in prehistory, the ancient Olympiads and modern Olympics, and so on.

Didactic approaches

No specific didactic approaches are proposed other than student-centred teaching and learning actively to master knowledge. Teachers are advised to employ alternate approaches flexibly and to connect history to students' knowledge from other disciplines. This is central to the recent cross-thematic curricular reforms. Approaches include the use of narratives, dialogues, the use of sources through documents and artefacts, individual and group work and visits to sites and museums.

Evaluation

As with didactic approaches, there is variety in forms of evaluation. Methods are suggested to evaluate students' knowledge and competences, but also for teachers to examine their own teaching. Oral and written work contributes to formative and cumulative assessment through examinations, individual project work and portfolios.

Educational materials

The educational materials to be used include student textbooks, teachers' guidebooks (one for every grade) and supportive additional material such as interactive CDs, DVDs, historical maps and collections of images. As this chapter was being written, the texts, guides and supportive materials for both Elementary Gymnasium grades were being prepared, following extensive guidelines and seminars for authors organised by the Hellenic Pedagogical Institute (PI) of Greece. This is the advisory body of the Ministry of Education and Religious Affairs, responsible for curricula, textbooks and the evaluation of education and in-service training of teachers. The materials are being prepared by those applicants who were ranked highest in terms of academic quality through a process of blind review and evaluation of sample materials.

Some materials will be ready and the new curriculum will begin in the academic year 2006-2007. Hitherto, a single textbook has been used throughout the country, largely for financial reasons. There are problems in relying on a single book, so the new materials will combine historical narrative with additional materials such as excerpts of written sources, different interpretations and contrasting comments, maps, diagrams, illustrations and photographs, glossaries and a bibliography of books appropriate to the level of students' development. This will be far superior to the textbooks currently in use. These moves to counter the effect of using just one textbook are fundamental to the cross-curricularity in the PI guidance. Authors were advised to use rich and varied supportive material, including literature, works of arts, photographs, films and contrasting interpretations of the same event, in order to give to the history teacher access to exciting and thought-provoking materials for students. This is linked to the policy of moving from single, self-contained subjects to a horizontal alignment across disciplines and subjects.

Discussion
The State, the nation and history teaching
Greek society has a particular interest in research and teaching in history, and these subjects are sensitive. In Greece, identity is aligned with deep political convictions and related concerns with ethnicity, so history and its teaching is always a topic of interest.

Ethnicity in its varied conceptions is a central characteristic of modernity. The relationship of ethnicity and state can be seen as guaranteeing political independence and territory when ethnicity and state coincide as a geographical entity. The notion of ethnicity is analysed from two central perspectives. The first gives precedence to the political programme and political power in which the State is the main factor in ethnic homogenisation and ethnic conscience. Ethnicity is a state political ideology in this framework. The second perspective gives precedence to ethnotic and national identities as cultural and social entities and procedure. This reveals a dynamic field of negotiations around the meaning of ethnotic and national symbolism, which also considers factors such as race, gender and social class (Gazi, 2004).

The notions of ethnic identity and patriotism

Globalisation – cultural, economic, demographical exchanges beyond national borders – has influenced the meaning of ethnic and national identity. Ideas of multiculturality were included in definitions of national identity in the European Union and the United States in the 1980s, giving a different perspective to patriotism, striving to harmonise the protection of national interests with the interests of humanity (Laliotou, 2004).

Yet the ethnic state is still recognised as protecting sovereignty and political rights. Ethnic states and ethnic national identities have been paradigmatic forms of modernity and have a central position in the world, despite the meaning of the term having evolved to include notions of interculturality, gender and/or class.

Faced with the globalisation of the economy, increasing mobility of populations and the growth of inter-ethnicity relationships, societies in the 21st century need to develop new ways of analysing and dealing with power relationships and new conceptions of citizenship and of political rights. The tension between a patriotism – conceptualised as national pride in the Greeks' contribution to humanity, which tends to minimise the contribution of others – and a broader patriotism oriented to humanistic ideas, was evident in older Greek history textbooks. After many historical tragedies and through the influence of the Council of Europe, textbooks became less nationalistically oriented.

There are a plethora of challenges faced by the new curriculum and the new textbooks in teaching history in Greece. Three particular problems have been selected for brief examination in this chapter: how the Turks and the Ottoman Empire are approached in the texts currently in use; the role of the Greek Orthodox Church in the formation of Greek identity; and the presentation of the Greek Civil War-related stance of Greece towards the Soviet Union in the 1980s and 1990s.

Turkish occupation in Greek textbooks

Greek-Turkish relations are an issue that has often found expression in the sphere of national identity formation, as well as in European Union and Balkan history. In the light of what we have presented above as the aims of teaching history, it is relevant to examine how Turks and the Ottoman Empire, which dominated the Balkans for centuries, are portrayed in Greek history textbooks. The question has concerned researchers in Greece for years, particularly in the last decade. Petridis, Dragona and Askouni, who analysed Greek texts in the Southeast European Joint History Project, maintain:

> Despite the changes in the last twenty years, in the Greek textbooks there are still negative attributions to the Turkish people. Most of these negative attributions are included in the textbooks of the Gymnasium, and they almost all concern the Ottoman Turks, characterised as 'Asian conquerors', and 'adventurers' who conquered Byzantium by chance.

> The spreading of the Ottoman Turks in the Balkans ended with the occupation of Constantinople, followed by 'a cruel tyranny of the Turks', 'a dark period of slavery', and 'unaccountable suffering caused by the Turkish occupation'.

> The whole period of the Ottoman rule is described as disastrous for Hellenism. 'The burst of Ottoman invasion in the Byzantine territories of Asia Minor at the end of the 13th century, the taking of the Thracian city of Kallipolis in 1354, and finally the fall of the Byzantine Empire in 1453, have been the beginning of misfortune that put in danger the mere existence of the Greek nation'. The 'consolidation of the Ottoman rule over the Greek land had disastrous consequences for the Greeks', since it was followed 'by the painful darkness of the fall of Constantinople', by 'the slaughtering, the pillage, and the economic misery'. (2001, p14)

Dragona and Frangoudakis argue that, as well as explicit values, there are implicit meanings found in history books, due mainly to omissions. They point out:

> The books contain no information whatsoever on the education, literature, arts, or any cultural achievements of the Ottoman Empire although they include intellectual and artistic achievement of the

'Arab world'. The information on the military strength and the supremacy of power, together with the complete absence of mention of culture, produce a latent but strong derogatory message, that the Ottomans were forceful and fearful warriors, but an uncivilised and crude people. (2001, p43)

Petridis *et al* go on

The image of the Turks, indirectly painted by all the above, is negative, since they are a people first invading European territories, and then obstructing the Christian populations in the Balkans from following the important European developments in the political, economic, intellectual and artistic sphere. The definite impression given to the Greek student is that the Ottoman Empire has caused the Greek people an important delay in the course of European development since Europe was their natural environment, contrary to the Turks, coming from Asia. (2001, p14)

Carras (2001, 11) explained this as a result, among other factors, of the circumstances that led to the creation of nations in the Balkans in general.

Most textbooks and history teaching in the region, as elsewhere, have been developed as part of a massive enterprise of creating nation-states. It is not therefore surprising that there has been a tendency to stress what may be considered admirable in one's own country's history, but to give less attention to or exclude altogether elements of which one may be less proud. Where historical accounts refer to the other, particularly those others against whom the national group had been defined, there has been an inevitable tendency to include the less admirable and exclude some of the more positive elements. The results of such a double process of selective exclusion and inclusion contributes to national stereotyping of young people, which remains a major element of adults' judgments as active citizens.

The new textbook guidelines give specific directions to avoid derogatory characterisations and to give the facts as objectively as possible. Aspects of Balkan history, in which Greece fought bloody wars, should be included. These textbooks are in preparation for the school year 2006-2007.

Koulouri refers to the larger Balkan situation:

> The Balkan experience does not leave much room for optimistic answers. Although the *topoi* of national imagination differ from one country to the next (for instance, it is a battle in Serbia, a series of political events in Romania, an emblematic figure for Turkey and the classical past for Greece), many structural components of the national narratives are the same. The worship of memory but also the oblivion of painful events, the exaltation as well as the victimisation of the nation, the particular projection of the past onto the mirrors of the present and the future are features common in most Balkan countries. In ex-communist countries in particular, the rewriting of history after 1989 follows multiple and contradictory paths, from historical relativism to the anatomy of the national stigma. (Koulouri, 2002, p11)

[See also Murgescu and Mihalache, Chapter 4 in this volume).

The Orthodox Church, national identity and history teaching

The relationship of national Greek identity, Orthodox Christianity and the Greek Orthodox Church is a very complex issue, due in part to the historical circumstances of the creation of the modern Greek state.

Greek national identity crystallised around two different views. The first was the nation-state of the Enlightenment, developed by Plethon Gemistos and his conception of returning to ancient Greek civilisation. This led to an excessive adoration of ancient Greece and classicism. This was supported by members of the rising bourgeois classes, educated mainly in Western Europe by followers of the Enlightenment. The second view had its spiritual centre in Constantinople, now Istanbul, the heart of a Christian οικουμένη [*ikumeni*] within a superethnic vision. This view was supported by the Greek Orthodox Church. Petrides describes the way history textbooks present the role of the Church after the fall of the Byzantine Empire and the Turkish occupation of Greece:

> The Orthodox Church and particularly the Patriarchate, using the privileges accorded by Mohamed the Conqueror, renewed by his successors, became the centre of unity of Christian populations in

the Balkans, and especially the Greek populations. The privileges gave the Patriarch the role of 'a national leader', heading not only the Orthodox Church, but having moreover political responsibilities towards the Orthodox populations of the Ottoman Empire. (Petridis *et al*, 2001, p19)

Further, textbooks support the premise that the Orthodox Church conserved Greek culture:

While the Catholic Church was going through a deep crisis, because of the Reformation, and while the Renaissance, reinforced by Greek scholars, was spreading in the European area, in the ranks of the enslaved Hellenism, humble teachers, often monks or members of the clergy, were keeping alive the cultural and spiritual tradition of the Nation, or tried to transplant the Greek intellectual tradition in other Orthodox countries. (*ibid*)

According to history textbooks, the Greek Orthodox Church supported the efforts of the Greek National Revolution against the Turks, thus suggesting that there was no anticlericalism in Greece.

After the creation of the Greek state, the Greek Orthodox Church fervently supported the 'great idea' of expanding to include territories where Greek and Orthodox Christians lived: the idealised focus was on Constantinople and the Aghia Sophia, both sacred symbols of the past and lost glory of Byzantium and seen as part of the history of Greece.

The positions adopted over the relationship between Orthodoxy and Greek identity reflects the ideological stance of the researcher and writer. Those from the Greek Orthodox Church maintained that being Greek means being an Orthodox Christian. Others, more from the left, deny the relationship between the two. The prevailing perspective argues that the

... Orthodox Church maintained and saved not only the language but the identity itself of Greek people, whereas with the theology, anthropology, language, art, the liturgical time shaped the older and recent Greek culture, from the every day issues to the political organisation. (Kalaitzidis 2003, p63)

These special ties between Greek identity and the Orthodox Church led to the instrumentalisation of the Orthodox Church by the state: the Church supported the efforts of the state in a way that can be seen as an aberration from the ecumenical, supranational mission of the Church. Kitromilides (1998) and Yannaras (1986) are useful sources for following this complex and multifaceted issue in greater depth.

Current challenges in History teaching

The Greek Civil War was fought between 1945 and 1949, predominantly between the Greek Right Conservatives and Greek Leftists. Following World War II, in which many Greeks fought and died, the Civil War was a very difficult time in Greek history and affected the entire nation. Yet this period was not referred to in the content of school history. History teaching stopped at the Second World War. In the 1960s and 1970s, the communist guerrillas who had fought in the Civil War were referred to as gangsters (*symmoritis*), and an ideological war against communism was reflected in history textbooks. In the 1980s and 1990s, the ideology shifted, and the ideas and sympathies of the left gained momentum and changed the content of the textbooks. The Soviet Union was somewhat idealised and textbooks were written accordingly. For example, Kelpanides (2005) argues that the authors of the Greek gymnasium history textbook *Modern and Current History*, in a chapter on the rise of Bolshevism and the establishment of the communist regime in Russia, present an ideological and misleading view. He argues that the authors omit issues such as the death of millions from famine caused by collectivisation, violence against the peasants, violence against the church, the failure of agricultural policies, the pathology of the communist system, the suppression of other European nations under communist regimes and social and educational inequalities. He concludes that the authors this create an idealised image of the system and of the Soviet Union. This textbook is in use and Kelpanidis suggests that the way information is presented does not help students understand either the rise or the fall of Communism regime in the Soviet Union.

Epilogue

The fluctuation of ideological tides and the way in which past authors presented relations between forces and institutions are not the only challenge in history teaching in Greek secondary schools. The authors of the new books must find a delicate balance between the national identity and European and global identity, between the description of a very long past and the analysis of urgent contemporary issues, and between traditional abstract learning and experiential approaches. The need to develop critical thinking and actively engaged citizens means that schools must see the teaching of history as a critical field of the curriculum.

To paraphrase our title, we conclude by suggesting that history teaching in schools today has as important role to play in the development of educated and well-informed citizens as it did when Laurie wrote in 1900:

> [history] is the introduction of the young mind to the record of the past of the race to which he himself belongs, and whose traditions it will be his duty to pass on to the next generation. It would be to waste words to endeavour to show how closely the study of this record is associated with moral training in the altruistic virtues, and with that kind of political instruction that best fits the rising generation for the discharge of their duties as citizens in one commonwealth. It strengthens the sympathy of man with men and binds more closely the social bond. By the study of past greatness, moreover, we learn to strive to be worthy of our forefathers, and, by the understanding of the causes which have so often led mankind astray, we learn to understand better the questions which arise in our own time, and to act during the brief period assigned to us on the stage of life with circumspection and under a sense of responsibility to those who are to succeed us. (Laurie, 1900)

The actualisation of this conception of teaching history depends on developing and implementing an appropriately constructed curriculum, training reflective and critical history teachers and employing teaching strategies and approaches that help students and future citizens to develop critical thinking skills. These skills and abilities are pivotal if students are to be in a position to reflect on and understand the past, live productively in the present and actively help to shape their future.

6

History and Civic education teaching, identities, and citizenship: a case study of Cyprus

Mary Koutselini

Introduction

The curriculum is not merely a definition of aims, methods, and content: it is primarily and *par excellence* a pedagogical text founded on political, ideological and sociological bases. Specific pedagogical, ideological, political and sociological choices are made in the identification of the subjects of study, their content, the time allotted to their study and the method and way in which they are assessed. The underlying pedagogical, political and sociological concepts pervading the curriculum are interrelated and inseparable. In this sense, the examination of the philosophical, political and social contexts, in both a broad and narrow sense, within which curriculum decisions are made, provides a firm basis for interpreting curriculum choices, textbook writing and educational policy. Curriculum, texts and policy indicate what kind of citizens we want our educational systems to develop.

This chapter is a case study of the History and Civic Education curriculum in Cyprus. An analysis of teaching and textbooks allows an exploration of the relationship between the strategies and models of teaching and the processes of identity-building through civic education, with particular reference to conflict-solving and inter-cultural education.

The curriculum documents for History and Civic Education in Cyprus provide important historical evidence for a hermeneutic understanding of social and political interests, the problems and the dilemmas in a country moving from colonial rule to membership of the European Union. Such an hermeneutic approach shifts the perspective of analysis of institutional historical change from the macro-level to the micro-level, by focusing on the roles of individuals and institutions in the community and society, as well as their dilemmas, attitudes, compromises, conflicts and interests.

A number of comparative studies underline the important role of context in citizenship education. It is generally agreed that schools prepare students for their role as citizens and teach them about their reciprocal rights and obligations, but there is no agreement on the content of civic education or the processes through which the balance of rights and duties are internalised. A consequence of this is that curricular requirements for civic education vary between countries (Torney-Purta and Schwille, 1986; Torney-Purta *et al*, 1999; Kerr, 1999). Tradition, geography, socio-political and economic structures and global trends have been suggested as principal contextual factors influencing citizenship education (Kerr, 1999, p5), and also the concept of citizenship itself (Koutselini, 2000).

Citizenship is a relationship between the individual and the state which binds both together through reciprocal rights and obligations. But the meaning of rights and obligations in this context remains an issue of debate that is currently of topical interest in many countries. In this context, the concept of citizenship has been defined broadly as social and moral responsibility, community involvement and political literacy, and it involves values to be internalised, skills to be acquired and knowledge to be taught in a multicultural society.

The Cyprus educational, social and political background: the divisive role of education

The Constitution imposed in 1960 on the newly established Republic of Cyprus recognised two different national communities, the Greek majority (80.1 per cent of the population) and the Turkish minority (18.6 per cent) (with a further 1.3 per cent of other minorities). This recognition was enhanced with special provisions to accommodate their different national characteristics. Education became the separate responsibility of the Greek Cypriot community and the Turkish Cypriot community through their respective Communal Chambers, rather than being the responsibility of the government of the Republic. The national mission of education for both communities enhanced the two communities at the expense of the national government.

Giving the Communal Chambers responsibility for providing education deepened the division between Greek and Turkish Cypriots. From 1960 to 1974, both Greek and Turkish public schools in Cyprus had ethnic education as their primary aim. There was a radical change following the island's invasion and partial occupation in 1974: the Cyprus Republic's major aim for education became the strengthening of Cyprus as an independent state, paralleled by the counter policy of the Turkish Cypriots in the occupied areas. Political and constitutional interests kept the two communities separate in different territories with restrictions to freedom and movement in the occupied areas.

The changes in the philosophy, aims and objectives of the curricula demonstrate a diachronic shift in the state's expectations of its citizens. These took shape under the influence of changing and historically specific objective conditions. As an example of this, the ideology of the government, teachers and students – and consequently the roles that each of these attributed to themselves and to others – and understandings of the function of education took on a particular form following Independence in 1960, which came after a period of prolonged foreign rule of the country and the demise of the unredeemed ideological dream of *Enosis* (unification with Greece).

From this standpoint, we can distinguish three major periods that affected education in Cyprus in different ways (Koutselini, 1997a; Koutselini and Maratheftis, 2000). Within the boundaries of these three historical phases, various models of curriculum development were shaped, each determined by an interpretation of the basic question: What kind of citizens do we want to develop? The periods and models are:

■ Between Independence and the Turkish invasion of Cyprus: the ethnocentric early modern model (1959 to 1974), in which the citizen was a carrier and dispenser of national ideology and identity

■ From the Turkish invasion to first application from membership of the European Union: the modern model (1974 to 1992); the sceptical citizen and the dilemmas of Greek and Cypriot identity

■ From application for membership to the European Union to full accession: the search for a balance between modern and humanistic models (1992 to 2005), the European citizen

What distinguishes Cyprus from most post-colonial educational systems is that education was given a divisive role in both communities, each of which worked separately to build their own nationalities.

Education in the Cyprus Republic is compulsory from the ages 6 to 15 and the system is highly centralised. All schools are accountable to the Ministry of Education and Culture: all schools run the same programmes and have the same curricula and textbooks.

Education is currently being reformed. A holistic reform of all levels of education was introduced in August 2004 under the title of 'Democratic and Humanistic Education in the Euro-Cypriot Society'. The Reform Committee's report (Ministry of Education, 2004) gave special attention to the upgrading of citizenship education in both primary and secondary schools, in all subjects and in school culture and organisation. It was emphasised that this must include education towards reconciliation with Turkish Cypriots.

History and civic education: curricula, teaching and textbooks

The aims and objectives of Cyprus education and citizenship

The Ministry of Education defined the aim of education and the profile of future citizens as follows:

> The general aim of education in Cyprus is the development of free and democratic citizens with a fully developed personality, mentally and morally refined, healthy, active and creative, who will contribute with their work and their conscientious activity in general to the social, scientific, economic, and cultural progress of our country and to the promotion of the cooperation, mutual understanding and love among people for the prevalence of freedom, justice and peace. (Ministry of Education, *Primary school curriculum*, 1994a, p13)

The basic objectives refer to education in humanistic values, which would provide the development of students able to function within a multicultural society and a knowledge-based economy, and able to reflect in a critical and philosophical manner. The educational philosophy of Greek Cyprus was officially described as modernised, correctly oriented, and flexible, which would thus constitute the required basis for the physical survival, social progress and prosperity of the people of Cyprus (Ministry of Education, 2004b). The stated objectives are that Cypriot education should take into account both the European and the global educational context and aim at responding effectively to the needs of the individual, Cypriot society and contemporary scientific and technological challenges.

The democratic school emphasises the rights and obligations of citizens in a democratic environment, so that each student participates in curricular, extra-curricular, and school-based activities. Multicultural education is supported through various measures, including language support for students from other countries (which means the learning of Greek as a second language) and measures to facilitate the smooth integration of groups with different cultural identities (Ministry of Education and Culture, 2004b).

Concepts such as democracy, democratic life and human rights, in formal declarations and in practice, are important elements of formal schooling practices and of the educational environment. This accords with the policies set out in *Democratic Education in Europe* (Official Journal of the European Communities, 2004), and includes student participation in school and social life. Political discussion is allowed in school, and the educational ethos encouraged is that active participation in common affairs is an obligation of the citizen and that the government is responsive to the wishes and claims of its citizens. Many students in Cyprus are members of the youth organisations of political parties: these special sections of political parties focus on issues that concern the young.

The curriculum and textbooks of History and Civic Education: the need of revision

The aims of civic education are achieved through all the subjects of the curriculum (Papanastasiou and Koutselini, 1999). In primary education, there are no defined teaching times for Civic Education: this takes place across subjects. Students are expected to respect fellow humans and to uphold human rights (Ministry of Education, 1994b). The introduction to the primary school textbook *Becoming a Good Citizen* (Ministry of Education, 1993) sets out that primary school children are the young citizens of the Republic of Cyprus and that it is necessary that they know their rights and obligations at school, in the family, in the village or parish where they live, and in the Cypriot State. From this, it should be clear that the democratic school places much emphasis on the rights and obligations of citizens within a democratic environment founded on the declaration of human rights.

In the *Gymnasium* (junior secondary school) civic education is taught as a separate subject in a 45-minute session for one semester. In the *Lyceum* (upper secondary education) civic education is taught as a subject for one semester in the fifth grade. Civic education introduces the concepts and the structure of social and political life, acquainting students with the fundamental functions of a democratic state and developing a sense of responsibility towards the state and society. It aims at acquainting students with the Cypriot form of government, helping them understand local and international organisations and institutions, developing positive attitudes towards their homeland and the world (Ministry of Education, 1991). Textbooks encourage small-scale research in areas such as environmental studies, science, helping people with special needs and the election of student councils.

History and Civic Education in primary schools are considered part of the Social Studies curriculum, together with Religion, Geography, and Environmental Studies. History is taught as a separate subject for two 40-minute periods each week in the third to sixth grades (ages from 9 to12). Teaching is based wholly on textbooks, although curriculum documents suggest that teaching resources should also include visits to primary resources such as monuments, archaeological sites and museums (Records of the Ministry of Education and Culture, 2001). Third-grade teachers use textbooks written in Cyprus by teachers working in the Curriculum Development Unit of the Pedagogical Institute. Fourth to sixth grade teachers use both Cypriot and Greek textbooks: the Ministry of Education explains this in a circular to schools (Records of the Ministry of Education and Culture, 2001):

> The Greek textbooks for History refer to the history of all the Greeks and therefore they cannot include the local history of Cyprus. The suggestion is to use supplementary material on Cypriot History, so that Cypriot and Greek history are combined, to promote the knowledge of historical events, to formulate common national conscience, and to inspire pride for our common national origin and respect for the history of other people.

The primary and secondary history textbooks refer to the same thematic content: Ancient History, Byzantine History and the Modern Age. All have the development of the Greek nation as a central theme. They present wars, fights, treaties, agreements and conventions, usually finishing with a chapter on civilisation and culture. Textbooks are structured to include presentations of principal events, historical sources and documentation, discussion topics and activities, followed by materials for evaluating learning. Classroom teaching follows the same pattern, covering the content: this is particularly so in the upper secondary grades (Lyceum fourth to sixth grades) where there is considerable pressure from final and external examinations leading to Higher Education.

Despite the stated intentions of the Ministry, a content analysis of some textbooks shows that these neither contribute to fulfilling the general aims of education nor implement the aims and objectives of civic education. A content analysis of primary school textbooks for civic education (Koutselini and Papanastasiou, 1997) revealed a deep discrepancy between the Ministry's proposed aims for civic education and textbooks and the practice of teaching in this area.

The main reason for this is the uncertainty of the political situation: both teachers and textbook writers are hesitant to deal with such important and sensitive issues. To take a specific example, the concept of cooperation dominates at the expense of possible discussion about consensus, conflict resolution, reform or change. What is missed is the important need to teach students that some problems have no easy answers in the areas of cooperation and tolerance: 'what looks like a good solution often has a negative impact on an important segment of the community' (Rowe, 1990, p44). A number of authors suggest forms of good practice in teaching issues that concern conflict. Mitchell and Quan (2001) propose teaching scenarios in which the ending is an unresolved conflict: students must work towards suggesting a solution, thus developing skills in conflict resolution. But teachers in Cyprus see their main aim as being to cover the content, and this only gives students superficial knowledge and tends to confirm stereotypes held in society and portrayed in textbooks.

Cypriot textbooks for History and Civics have not been replaced since 1980. Apple (1993) suggests that the curriculum can be seen primarily as a cultural, political and sociological text that reflects a country's historical context, peculiarities, and educational system. The curriculum reflects compromises made between interconnected interests and expresses the prevalent cultural model and ideology: this must particularly be evident in the ways that textbooks, unchanged for years, are interpreted.

In this sense, the curriculum has been used historically both to exercise social, economic and cultural control, and to produce and reproduce institutions and ideology. The tendencies and orientations of the curriculum through the history of education in Cyprus have illustrated this dynamic: how various and often antagonistic groups have contributed to curriculum formulation, and the compromises of conflicting interests, such as between Greek and Turks during the period of Turkish rule from 1570 to 1870, and between Church and the State during the period of British rule from 1878 to 1960. Within such a framework, the particular situation, socio-political and economic conditions and the dominant ideology are parameters that shape the curriculum and the epistemological assumptions on which its delivery is based.

It is accepted that Cyprus now needs to revise its curricula and textbooks with the objective of eliminating elements that contribute towards negative stereotypes, such as showing cruelty during wars between Greek, Turkish and English, and describing different religions as superior or inferior. There is agreement that the curriculum should demonstrate positive aspects of the different cultures and ways of life, and introduce elements that will promote tolerance and respect for the other culture (Ministry of Education and Culture, 2004a).

It is also now seen as important that the school curricula emphasise human rights education, and that this needs to begin with the education of teachers and trainers. These teachers have in their background traces of the whole role of education through the island's history: education that reproduces the national idea, the scepticism and dilemmas of Greek national identity and neo-Cypriot identity, and European identity as an inclusive umbrella for different identities in a multicultural society. It was seen as remarkable that the creation of a new nation-state was suggested again in the most recent *Report of the Committee for the Reconstruction of the Cyprus Educational System* (Ministry of Education and Culture, 2004a, p9, 22).

The recommendation of the European Union in 2001 (Rec 2001, p15, *Official Journal of the European Communities*, 2001) is a clear call for differentiated history teaching: it emphasises the creation of an active citizenship which tolerates and respects diversity, and does not stereotype crimes towards humanity. As Delors (1996, p49) pointed out 'History has often served to bolster a sense of national identity by highlighting differences and extolling a sense of superiority...'. The new common aim in teaching history in an inter-cultural society must be focused on those periods that contributed to the cultivation of the European conscience, and on a willingness to study different cultures. All this presupposes that teachers will be educated and trained in the new aims and objectives of history teaching.

Conflicts, interests, and citizenship in a multicultural society
Research into the curricula of primary schools (Persianis, 1981) and secondary schools (Koutselini, 1997a) in Cyprus shows how the island's particular circumstances, institutions and dominant ideo-logies formulated educational policy and how this policy was re-flected in the curricula. Local and international characteristics, his-torical circumstances, institutions and ideologies have all influenced both educational policy and societal expectations of education, in a manner that can be traced in the curricula and in teaching.

The strong link between citizenship as meaning an obligation to national ideals and citizenship as enshrining culture is a demon-stration of the contemporary Cypriot fear that Greek identity is threatened. This fear has a long history, based on centuries in which education cultivated the national Greek identity. In the years before independence, and many of those after, education was the vehicle of national identity and was an implicit and explicit aim of schooling, especially during the years of foreign rule. This feeling intensified immediately after the Turkish invasion of 1974, when a resolution of the Cyprus problem based on the idea of a neo-Cypriot identity and ideology appeared, with some diminution of national identity (Kout-selini, 1997b, p403). This neo-Cypriot concept was based on the feeling that the problems of Cyprus were a consequence of this idea of national identity and of the dream of *Enosis*; it was therefore reasoned that, to co-exist peacefully in Cyprus, Greek and Turkish Cypriots needed to forget their separate identities and create a new

nation: unfortunately only Greek-Cypriots participated in this movement. This Neo-Cypriot ideological identity created further conflict
between Greek-Cypriots, both because of the attempt to alter the
national identity and because the cultivation of Turkish ethnic ideology in the occupied areas strengthened the Greek Cypriot national
feeling.

Issues of nationalism and regionalism have been critical in Cyprus
and have dominated discussions on citizenship education. After
1974, there was an attempt to base educational policy on demo-
cratisation rather than on national identity (Ministry of Education,
1993). In primary and secondary Civic Education textbooks, the
concepts of state and of nation were differentiated so that students
could understand that an independent state of Cyprus need not conflict with the Greeks of Cyprus feeling a Greek national identity
(Ministry of Education, 1993, 1994b). Cypriot citizenship has not
corresponded with the national identities of its people for some time
now. Different communities have had different political perspectives: unification with Greece for the Greek-Cypriots, and *taxim* (or
division into two independent states) for the Turkish-Cypriots. It is
for this reason that issues of nationalism and regionalism have been
crucial.

Since the accession of Cyprus to the European Union, this conflict
between national identities seems to have been clarified under conventions and recommendations of the EU that set out the goals of the
Union's policy: respect for human rights and fundamental freedoms,
the promotion of solidarity and support between nations and different nationalities (The Council of Europe, 1996; European Council, Official Journal C325, 2002; Commission of the European Community, 1995). It is now a time to understand – and through education, internalise – the idea that if 'we are at the same time more
aware of differences we become 'less different'' (Ross, 2000, p39).

The question remains: what is an intercultural education? The *All
equal, all different* educational pack developed by the European
Youth Centre (The Council of Europe, 1995) gives suggestions for
education against racism, xenophobia and intolerance. The authors

define multiculturalism by explaining how the term refers to different cultures, national, ethnic and religious groups, all living within the same territory but not necessarily coming into contact with each other. Intercultural societies refer to different cultures and groups that are able to maintain open relationships of interaction, exchange and mutual recognition of their respective values and ways of life. Intercultural processes presuppose the elimination of prejudice and stereotypes about other groups, and education can play an important early role in this.

But what of the dominant cultural pattern of each society within the nation? What about schooling in a state which has more than one dominant cultural model? In these cases, conflict about national identity has become a conflict of interest around political power (as in the case of Cyprus), which has led to separate schooling and the cultivation of different national identities within a common supra-European identity.

It is noteworthy that education for intercultural citizenship in a multicultural society presupposes practices and programmes for conflict prevention, such as those within the frame proposed for different levels by the European Commission (European Commission, 2001): that of individual members, content, interaction, the procedural level and the level that governs external relations with the environment. Each level is a potential source of conflict, and therefore a starting point for conflict resolution.

Conclusion

Cypriot education presents a unique case of a country with an educational policy that markedly divides its communities rather than unifying them. Any analysis must take into account the policy of the state and the various philosophical schools of educational policy, and also the particularly static model of educational culture which unyieldingly resists any form of educational change that might alter the nation's cultural model.

Epistemological, scientific and economic factors increase their influence over the curricula and extra-curricular activities. Whilst the national ideal is no longer the predominant aim of education, and curricular subjects are changing, the cultivation of national teachers and the survival of Greek civilisation in Cyprus remain among the main objectives of education. The task of studying and understanding the systems that control the curricula of countries with political problems that have appeared to have no long-term solution presupposes a study of context, as this may provide some understanding of this persistence of an unyielding national educational culture.

The analysis of History and Civic Education curricula, texts and underlying educational policies suggests that both Greek and Turkish Cypriots have mental states that remain deeply attached to the problem of the national. The social and psychological aspects of peace-building suggest the importance of examining social psychological impacts of conflict on individuals and society (see, for example, the John Hopkins Centre for International Studies, www.csis.org). If psychology drives the attitudes and behaviour of individuals and their collectivities, then it is important to understand the psychology of conflict and its consequences. Past traumas create suspicion that can prevent change. Both perspectives are legitimate, but neither side is willing to acknowledge the legitimacy of the other's claim. Conflict is the expression of deep fears, built on historical experience, in which each side sees the existence of the other as a threat to their own continuation.

The most important factor in citizenship education in Cyprus is the national political problem: students' understanding and education of conceptions of citizenship are strongly linked to this. European citizenship does not offer a harmonisation of understanding citizenship, because the political, social, economic and educational realities in the different countries imply different discourses, experiences and internalisation of the same concepts.

The problem with citizenship education is that it is difficult to foster respect of equity and difference at the same time; these issues both relate to power and how this can be controlled. Who has the power in citizenship education in Europe? Who should have the power and how can equality be achieved, between different countries as well as within one country with different cultures?

Healthy citizenship education demands the construction of a robust political philosophy that can provide new grounds for consensus, in place of traditional conflicts between individual freedom and social solidarity, state power and personalisation. Citizenship education for Europe is a quite different issue from citizenship education in Europe. The transcendence of specific characteristics of nationality does not imply the elimination of national identities, but the acceptance of multiple identities (regional, national, European, international), which support tolerance towards contrasting views, foreigners, minorities, and different cultures and religions.

7

The contribution of history to citizen education: Historiographical analysis and reflections on teaching citizenship

Concha Maiztegui Oñate and
Maria Jesús Cava Mesa

It is a devastation; in Spain the people are an electoral and taxable mass. As they are not loved, they are not studied; and as they are not studied, they are not known so that they may be loved. Miguel de Unamuno (1914, p71)

E ducation for citizenship is one of the modern grand narratives of education, providing a utopian path for individuals to become active citizens who are conscious of their rights and duties. These responsible citizens will have the necessary capacities and awareness to participate in public life, at both local and global levels (Council of Europe, 2001). This narrative and general orientation makes sense of and directs social debate (Gimeno Sacristán, 2003). The approaches of the disciplines of history, political sciences, education and sociology provide the essential reference points, and their perspectives influence both educational policies and practices. Practical applications are made in different areas of curriculum, including the teaching of history which, among its functions, includes the education of real citizens (Kennedy, 1991). History constitutes a particularly interesting discipline within which to develop the competences necessary for citizenship, since it contributes to the diffusion of a common narrative of the past and the present, making it possible to reconstruct a lucid vision of society and the world. Its teaching permits, potentially, the development of different dimensions of citizenship: the personal, the temporal, the spatial and the social (Cogan and Derricott, 1998).

The first part of this chapter presents an approach to the idea of citizenship in Spanish historiography. The second part reviews citizenship education within social science education in schools.

The idea of citizenship in Spanish historiography

We must begin this outline of the development of the concept of citizenship in Spanish historiography by acknowledging that there are very few significant sources on the subject. Some recent comparative examples explore how Spanish society has, since the early 19th century, rooted and articulated an enlightened form of citizenship within institutional structures common to other countries in emancipated Europe. This long historical process is an established element of the country's historical interpretation.

Most writers have properly criticized those governments that did not acknowledge the need for systems of justice, or the legitimate aspirations of men and women to be citizens, rather than subjects. This basic narrative, now diversified into many academic dimensions, still leaves a lacuna concerning specific studies of citizenship *per se*. There are very few specific studies of the development of civic rights in Spain, or of the role of the citizen in the political system and society and, because of this gap, the historical development of the concept of citizenship must be traced through references to democratic and ant-democratic phases in our history. There are only brief references in specialist journals, and occasional indications in courses and seminar series. Historical sociology is the discipline most able to contribute usefully to this gap.

Although there is evidence of the development of citizenship (sometimes of a progressive nature) in Spanish socio-political culture in our recent history, the concept as such did not receive definitive recognition until the 1990s, when a compelling awareness of the need for citizenship arose as the great economic, social and political changes that had begun in 1976 became embedded.

Citizenship is understood as the legal and political status by which the citizen acquires individual rights (civic, political, social) and has to undertake duties (of good faith, military service, etc.) in a relationship with the political collectivity, and to participate in the communal life of the state. Citizenship arises out of the principle of democratic popular sovereignty and, in Spain, as in many other countries, was a constituent of the idea of the nation-state, reinforced by the welfare state.

One of the concerns of contemporary citizenship is how to maintain previously agreed minimum levels of social welfare in the face of internationalisation and the relaxation and deregulation of the economy that is associated with globalisation. This concern makes it necessary to transcend the ideas of the rights and duties of citizenship within a national border towards a more holistic concept, progressing towards a global citizenship in which citizenship is not merely limited to the political rights and obligations of a legal or constitutional relationship with a territory.

Nevertheless, citizenship today (and European citizenship) still has its origins in the city, and was the characteristic of the status-free men and women. Rights and duties were entrenched in the institutions for representation and government at local level: city councils that exercised control through the elected assembly were the precursor of full political democracy. Citizens were the inhabitants of the city in law, and even today the population in each Spanish municipality is distinguished between the population in law and in fact. As Cortina (1997, p34) notes: 'citizenship is primarily a political relationship between an individual and a political community, by virtue of which the individual is a full member of that community and owes permanent loyalty to it'. The concept of citizenship thus (at least in the West) regulates the permanent tension or balance between the need for social unity and the need to separate from others.

Aristotle, in Book III of *The Politics* (1992) refers to the nature of the city and being a citizen: the citizen is defined by nothing better than by participation in the administration of justice and government – thus denying the validity of the two criteria for citizenship commonly invoked by later legal traditions, by residence (*ius soli*) or by descent (*ius sanguinis*). A citizen is simply a person with the capacity to participate effectively in the government of the city. The present concept of citizenship began with the appearance of the modern state, related to both parts of the term nation-state – that is to say, 'state' and 'nation'.

This premise for the liberal tradition of citizenship is elementary but inevitable, relating ideological and social movements to the post-1800 historical narrative and the economics of modernisation, shared by many European societies, including that of Spain.

The concept of state refers to a form of political organization that was formed in Europe from the 13th century until the end of the 18th or the start of the 19th, and which from there extended throughout the civilised world, freeing itself to an extent from the specific conditions of its birth (Cortina and Conill, 2001).

Javier Peña (2000, p73) reminds us:

> although the roots of citizenship are Greek and Roman, the present concept of citizenship comes mainly from 17th and 18th centuries, from the French, English and American revolutions, as well as from the birth of Capitalism.

But, in the words of Pérez Ledesma (2000, p40):

> our perception of ancient and, in general, historical citizenship, is, in principle, inseparable from the representation that we make of contemporary democracy, of our own anthropology of the citizen and of the political order in which we develop.

These two experiences of citizenship had been conceived from the 18th century in a politico-legal sense. The French Revolution invented the more modern conception, and it was this that permeated the Spanish constitutionalism of the 19th century. Pérez Ledesma (2000) suggests that this innovation operated on at least three levels: legal citizenship (equal citizenship before the law, in contrast to former local or statutory privileges); political citizenship (the citizen as a member of the political and participative body in public affairs); and national citizenship (the citizen as integrated in the state, compared to his or her previous relationship with intermediate bodies, and, at the same time, separated radically from the foreigner). But Pérez Ledesma also argues:

> in the second of those senses ... the invention met with special difficulties, derived from the resistance between two different conceptions of citizenship, one of which enjoyed the prestige of a long history while the other was just beginning to arise in the revolutionary process itself. (2000, p120)

The Spanish representatives who met in the Cortes of Cadiz faithfully followed the French tradition. The Constitution of 1812 – as did the French text of 1791 – established a sharp separation between Spaniards and citizens. 'All free men born and domiciled in the dominions of Spain ... plus foreigners who obtained naturalization papers, could enjoy the condition of Spaniards, and with her of 'civil freedom, property and other legitimate rights" (Pérez Ledesma, 2000, p121). But some Spaniards were excluded from being citizens, such as domestic servants, Spaniards of African origin, unemployed people and the illiterate.

Only citizens could elect, or be elected, for municipal office or as representatives. In the Constitution of Cadiz the distinction between 'civil citizenship' and 'political citizenship', or between 'naturals' and 'citizens', appeared as in the French Constitution of 1791, though reflecting the different structure and social composition of the Spanish state. Civil rights were common for all individuals through natural law, but political rights were limited and granted only for 'the general good and the different forms of government"(Pérez Ledesma, 2000, p121).

In the history of the Spanish constitution, the absence of a stable constitutional pact led to some notable failures in citizenship awareness, particularly during the Carlist wars of 1833 to 1876. The political functions of the Constitution that identified the powers and rights of the citizen were both basic and traumatic. As Zamora notes (2001), the constitutional pendulum in Spanish history was not a consequence of any 'special idiosyncrasy of the Spanish' that made them incapable of reconciling liberalism and democracy. The rights of the citizen were key to the political system:

> between 1834 and 1874 the liberals completed the work of Cadiz and the Triennium on this point, following a substantially identical process to that followed in Europe, in this task of the identification of 'man' with 'citizen'. (Rodríguez, 2005, p38)

But the restricted suffrage was challenged as a basis of sovereignty, as in the revolution of 1868 (just as it had been in France in 1848). The 1869 constitution (articles 16-20) confirmed this, albeit only temporarily. The constitution of the 1874 restricted suffrage, to the extent that, when there was a return to universal masculine suffrage in 1890, the electoral roll increased six-fold. Alvarez Junco (1998) highlights the difficulty in classifying the Spanish political system during the Restoration in terms of either modernity or traditionalism. Recent historical writing characterises the late 19th and early 20th century period as that of 'a society in transition' (Alvarez Junco, 1998; Juliá, 1998). 'This is a country in which a centralized, modern, nation state has been constructed, but on paper, more than in reality' (Alvarez Junco, 1998, p73; Juliá, 1998, p73). Juliá (1998) characterises Spain at this time as premodern, given the state's incapacity to define law or to exercise control, with the endemic political domination and influence of *caciques* (local political leaders) in which decisions had to be negotiated with local powers. Democratic participation and inclusiveness were absent and universal suffrage, despite its re-emergence in 1890, was ineffective.

This was not, from any liberal perspective, a free society, and the rights of the citizen were notable for their absence. This was particularly so in the countryside, where liberties were taken advantage of, figuratively and literally. Political culture was deficient, and the norms, beliefs and values of citizenship were invisible at many points. Spanish citizenship pursued its ideals in a particular and different way (Juliá, 1998, p159). The residual effects of the society of this old regime meant that, at the end of the 19th century, Spain was dissected by diverse conflicts – mythification, demystification, centralisation, decentralisation, clericalism, anticlericalism, nationalism, regeneration – particularly after the Spanish-American war, the disaster of '98. Citizenship was plunged into a great ocean of uncertainty, which persisted until the socio-political landmark of the Second Republic in 1931. The historical corollary soon materialised in the civil war.

The generation of '98 were the intellectuals and writers who contributed to 'the glorious resurrection of Spain', but their texts were loaded with anthropological pessimism. Civilization was something coercive, wrote the Basque philosopher Unamuno (1914). But he also wrote (during a phase of popular action) that 'Spain is about to be discovered and only Europeanised Spaniards will discover it' (Unamuno 1914, p85), arbitrarily identifying awareness – just as Tuñón de Lara (1986) avoided it – with Europeanisation. He emphasised the role not only of intellectual or political elites, but also that of citizens.

The Decree of 8 May 1931 extended suffrage to the clergy and women, confirming their rights as citizens to stand for election. Universal suffrage, without class distinction, was finally confirmed in the Constitution of 9 December 1931. This social reinforcement of citizenship can be seen in Balado (2003):

> the attempts to establish a 'national education' were in our country a praiseworthy effort to bring the light of science and culture to all, and with them, the intellectual emancipation that the democratic system demands, when this was based on a 'metaphysics of subjectivity', that is to say, the fortification of the individual as the main political and social creator ... To associate education, culture, democracy and freedom, was and remains a precondition for forging a political system, such as the democratic one, whose health and vigour are based on the quality of its citizens.

The impact of the civil war gave modern citizenship in Spain as *an also unpredicted* consequence, a result of warlike conflict that broke the stability of the *status quo* (Pérez Ledesma, 2000, p143).

Union and labour struggles and a coalition of pressure groups during the course of much of the 20th century led governments to reform and improve political rights. The rejection of class struggle also modified the process of construction of citizenship.

The so-called organic democracy of Francoism left this citizenry in a state of meagre representation, participation being restricted to collective formulas and official corporations. Citizens were sometimes consulted in extraordinary circumstances, for example, over the Law of Succession of 1947 and the Statutory Law of the State in 1967. These plebiscites, which approved the proposals of the Regime by acclamation, cannot be compared to the democratic expression of opinion. The decisive step that initiated change towards a constitutional project came later, with a representative regime based on civic participation.

The Constitution of 1978 was the result of a history of bitter misunderstandings between Spaniards. It incorporated Spain into modernity (Balado, 2003), and any evaluation of its values, rights and liberties must be made in the context of the country's past. The concept of citizenship has become denser as it has developed, and its scope and content mark the political fluctuations through which Spain has passed. New social pacts at the global level have also had their effects on our society and its citizens. The appearance of diverse citizens is another aspect of the contemporary world that has had its effect. The new working citizenship, with its incorporation of women and its recognition of autonomies, has its roots in years of social struggle and conflict. In the edited collection *Citizenship and Democracy*, the sociologist Valiente (2000) identifies the influence of notions of equality in the establishment of social rights of women as citizens, tracing the successful strategies that started in the 1980s, from the creation of the Institute of the Woman in 1983 and the ensuing legislation.

The relationship between European citizenship and national citizenship is a terrain especially cultivated by politicians and sociologists: Spain, having passed the phase of transition to democracy, is now a member of the European Union.

Peña limits the present idea of citizenship: 'In my opinion, the most notable aspects of the concept of citizenship are participation, rights and belonging' (2001, p25). Citizenship as a political ideal with strong liberal roots owes much to the influence of T. H. Marshall (1950), spread by contemporary conservative and neoliberal writers; an important gloss was given by Pérez Ledesma (2000). But globalisation has presented a new set of problems: deficiencies in the ideal of the citizen appear less significant as new tensions appear, among others, of migration.

For many decades, as has been noted, the concept of citizenship has been restricted. Many writers now elaborate citizenship in non-formal democratic contexts within the principles of the western liberal tradition. The resurgence of citizenship can be explained both on the level of theory and of experience of socio-political life in contemporary societies.

At the level of theory, citizenship is intimately bound to the idea of the citizen's inherent individual rights and to the notion of a bond with a particular community and participation in that community's public-political sphere. In this sense, citizenship appears bound to specific anthropological conceptions, as both a set of inalienable rights and the exercise of virtues, obligations and responsibilities towards other members of the civic community. At the level of social experience, interest in citizenship has been fed by political events and trends taking place all over the world.

The vigour and stability of a modern democracy do not only depend on the justice of its 'basic structure' (Rawls, 1971), but also on the dispositions, links, practices and attitudes of its citizens. For example: citizens' feelings of identity and their perception of the potentially conflicting forms of national, regional, ethnic or religious identities; their capacity to accept and work with diverse individuals; their motivations to associate with strangers; their disposition to-

117

wards change, flexibility and innovation; their desire to participate in the political process to promote the public good; their disposition to limit themselves and to exert personal responsibility in economic demands, in their dealings with family and neighbours, and in environmental questions and sustainable development.

These variables can be clearly ordered around specific problems and interpretations of citizenship itself, and the assertions of citizenship by the diverse members of Spanish society (Habermas, 1992). Spanish citizenship now faces a double challenge. There are factors that put the acquired content of citizenship at stake and, against these, there are new phenomena that extend the contents and renew the concept of citizenship. As in other European countries, a growing number of the population are progressively losing their attributes as citizens: they do not vote, they do not have work, they live in marginal areas, they feel excluded from institutions, and they are not connected with communication networks; they are outside, which is worse than being underneath.

Recent analyses of these aspects centre on dimensions that, beyond European literature and its project of citizenship, reflect on symptoms of change and extension (Cortina, 1999; Peña, 2000; Pérez Ledesma, 2000). These writers identify:

- the need for universal rights that guarantee the protection of the environment, access to new communication technologies, and public services under private management

- the feminine redefinition of citizenship, based on legal, social, political and cultural equality between genders

- the expansion of citizenship to non-nationals, or access to nationality, multinationality or the separation of citizenship and nationality

- cultural identity as a component of citizenship, as a civic counterweight to globalisation

- the right to the city, when suburbanisation and exclusion deny basic rights to economic integration, political participation, cultural socialisation, personal security, access to work, mobility and to recognition by others

In conclusion, citizenship today is affected by dizzying and unpredictable changes in society: technological changes, changes in family and social structure, changes in the values that govern the conduct of young people and adults. Whether changes are superficial or profound, it is necessary to define what essentially marks humanity, and thus the ethical roots of education: there is a strong connection between ethical education and citizenship education.

Teaching History and Citizenship Education[1]

Compulsory education in Spain lasts from six to sixteen years of age. The first four years of secondary education (12 to 16 years) are divided into two compulsory two-year cycles, followed by two elective years that allow direct university access. This aligns the start of the citizen's working life with other countries in the European Union.

The Ministry of Education identifies the characteristic pedagogy of this stage as personalised and comprehensive learning. The Ministry's plan for curriculum diversity and secondary integration was expected to facilitate pupils' integration through educational provision adapted to meet the needs of each individual. Different educational pathways, special education and training are provided for students of varying scholastic attainment and of different social origins, integrated in comprehensive schooling. As a component of citizenship, the form of teaching responds to the demand for fairness (Santibáñez and Maiztegui, 2004).

The increasing heterogeneity of schools has led to difficulties in creating a working environment that allows education to be adapted to the differing rates of learning of pupils (Marchesi and Martín, 2002). This is already becoming more difficult in secondary education, where students with learning difficulties, or those with low personal and family prospects, progressively lose interest in following the curriculum. It is during this stage that the Social Sciences, including geography and history, are introduced and given three hours of study each week. The objectives for this course include developing competences for inclusion in public life, such as self-guided learning and teamwork. The history syllabus over the two cycles covers prehistory and ancient history; medieval history, modern history and contemporary history.

The Spanish educational system combines national directives with a decentralisation to the seventeen autonomous communities that comprise the state. Thus the basic and common structure described above may be augmented by each autonomous community with curricular components on the geography and history of its region. Textbooks have two differentiated parts, one common and one adapted to the requirements of the autonomous region. Schools also have considerable autonomous powers in organising the curriculum. Some may alternate history and geography over the year, while others may teach just geography in the first cycle, followed by just history in the second cycle. Some teachers will begin their approach to history from understanding the contemporary world, moving backwards through time, while others will adopt a more traditional chronological approach starting with the earliest times.

The most recent curriculum revision from the Ministry of Education and Science, *An education of quality for all and among all* (2004), explicitly refers to citizenship education needing to develop the social values that will allow an active participation in a democratic society. Citizenship education is to take place in the final cycle of primary education, the two cycles of compulsory secondary education and the baccalaureate cycle, and to be the responsibility of the history teachers within the social sciences department.

Prior to this, citizenship education was integrated across the entire curriculum, described as a 'global project of humanisation' and a vertebral axis of transversality (Naval and Laspalas, 2000, p13). In practice, particularly at secondary level, it had become diluted, or simply forgotten when placed alongside traditional material (Anaut, 2002). The 2004 text implies a new approach, paralleling the activities of other European countries (Eurydice, 2004). Currently the educational system is in a period of analysis and debate about how to improve different educational agents.

The theory of citizenship education speaks of equipping people with the resources to participate in the public space (Banks, 1997). The process sets out the citizenship competences to be developed, specifying the knowledge, values, feelings and abilities necessary to actively participate in society (Bartolomé Pina, 2002; Council of Europe, 2001; Remy, 1998). One of the difficulties for teaching staff is to teach those abstract concepts which allow students to go beyond the data and to engage in sustained critical analysis (Pagès, 2005). For example, certain basic elements of citizenship, such as the concepts of democracy or citizenship, are studied at around 12 or 13 years of age, but sometimes pupils do not understand it in sufficient depth. While these concepts are related to each other, the divisions of the historical curriculum across school years means that each concept is developed in a different subject and year (for example, liberal revolutions and the citizen). Pupils may find difficulty in elaborating a vision that integrates these different courses and sets of knowledge.

This situation led to a team of teachers from the University of Murcia developing a didactic exposition for the democratic education of citizens in the compulsory phase of education (Albacete, Cárdenas and Delgado, 2000). This was based on key social concepts, allowing conventionally taught subjects to have a formative dimension, not simply informative.

Delgado points out that it is 'to a certain point paradoxical to initiate a process by which individuals must learn to be a citizen before they understand with depth and accuracy what the fact of being one constitutes' (Delgado, 2004, p37). They therefore present a synthesis of the concepts and values entailed in education for democratic citizenship. In the compulsory secondary education phase, the proposed objective is 'to understand and to assimilate that the identity as a citizen is composed of rights and duties and is rooted in participation, to the point that it is considered as the main mechanism of the democratic system' (Delgado, 2004, p42). Linked to this – and essential in citizenship – is the key concept of power, which is critical in the operation of all social groups. The final cycle (14 to 16 years) culminates in the development of the concept of the citizen, from the ancient Greeks to the modern world.

As noted earlier, increasing migration has presented new challenges to Spanish society and has influenced the debate on citizenship. In education, the most urgent adaptations have aimed at facilitating the integration of these diverse pupils through language classes and courses of reinforcement. But, as well as this, the education system has to offer a global perspective through analysing the socio-cultural context of migrations, sustainability and human rights. The didactic axes of the social sciences (territory, societies, cultures, history) can raise common questions on the different factors affecting the complexity of social life. In approaching certain historical subjects such as colonisation and the conquest of America, pupils will have diverse experiences and knowledge, with different narratives from the past and present. This cultural diversity supports studying the factors that condition and construct history and knowledge, and also gives the opportunity to discuss from alternative perspectives and to amplify the vision of historical events.

Textbooks have incorporated readings and reflective activities on matters related to citizenship, such as the rights of minorities, the situation of women or globalisation. This emphasis on inclusiveness is particularly relevant for citizenship education (Kennedy, 1991). However, despite the changes since the mid-Seventies, research shows there has been little change in how most texts explain thematic areas, and that an abundance of superficial descriptions continue (Argibai, Celorio and Celorio, 1991; Bastida, 1994).

Educational legislation in Spain includes certain common values for the state, but leaves the development of the details to the competent authorities (Kerr, 1999). This is an intermediate position: more explicit than those countries that have only minimum references in educational legislation but, because of our regional and school autonomy, less detailed than in Japan, Singapore, Korea or Sweden. In the Spanish case, greater specificity is found in the educational definition at school level, where each institution makes explicit its ideas and the type of citizens that it wishes to train. There is no specific examination or evaluation of these values and aspects; but the involvement of pupils in group activities, showing respect for others and the recognition of differences, is considered.

The need to increase social cohesion in post-industrial societies and to generate a common identity is one objective of citizenship education. The ethical dimension of citizenship thus implies an affective dimension, related to feelings of belonging. This concerns political and geographic aspects, with local identity but also with multiple identities that allow global identification with other, and with local and global groups. Being aware of co-responsibility for collective groups entails the ability to become involved and to make decisions.

But what values are appropriate for the cosmopolitan citizen? Cortina (1997) suggests that the core values of civic ethics are freedom, equality, solidarity – an active model, different from one based on economic and social success, patterns of consumption and disregard for social problems. To attain this active model, secondary teachers must know the values to teach and be convinced of their validity in order to transmit them to students and to evaluate them from a critical perspective. From such a perspective, the challenge is to require educators to learn and teach citizen values and to create a democratic atmosphere.

Such an education requires a substantial change in the way classes are taught, and in the management of schools. It requires the involvement of the teaching staff, who should not be limited to a set curriculum or text, but should look to new ways of working, using other resources, materials and aids. Another requirement is the inter-relationship of historical processes in a broad context, transcending the tendency to analyse different subjects separately. This does not always happen and, though this is not necessarily because of the school programmes, it continues in many textbooks and educational practice itself (*Asociación para la Enseñanza de la Historia*, 1998). On the other hand, the diversity of the pupils who embark on secondary education, as well as the basic education of the teaching staff (who must have both a four or five-year degree in a specialised subject and a teacher-training qualification from a University Institute of Education Science) and the structure of the centres makes this process difficult in secondary classes.

The teaching staff are key in introducing the learning and the experience of citizenship and identity in a European context. Different studies in this field all mention the need to educate teachers to be coherent in their teaching and for this to be integrated into their teacher training courses (Council of Europe, 2001).

In Spain, this has not yet become reality, but the continuing education of teaching staff has undergone great development. Conscious of its role in enhancing educational quality, the Departments of Education in the Autonomous Communities, the Ministry and Foundations such as Santa María and Santillana have invested in this area, often in collaboration with the Education Sciences Institutes of the local Universities, although the levels of secondary teacher education are still below those of other countries (Alvarez, 2002). Recently, topics such as conflict resolution and bullying in school have had attention: these subjects are important in citizenship education in a plural society.

The school is a microcosm of society in which to learn and practice citizenship, but this will only happen when the management, teachers and other staff give pupils the opportunity to do so. The involvement of parents and other social agents are also important elements in this (Eurydice, 2004). This type of education entails a restructuring of the system so that pupils are given the possibility to participate in decision-making in an open and democratic way (Council of Europe, 2001; Eurydice, 2004; Kennedy, 1991).

The autonomy of our schools and scholastic centres is relative, with direct control coming from the state and the autonomous authorities (García Garrido, 1987). But they do have some elements of representation of families and pupils, such as School Councils, where parents and pupils help elect the school management. Several recent interesting and innovative activities have aimed at renewing educational methodologies and managements, usually in primary training centres. Examples are the Atlantida project (*Proyecto Atlantida*) and the learning communities which model generator schools. Since 2000, the programmes of Educative Innovation of the Basque Government have been in operation (Departamento de Educación, 2004): these specify the responsibility of the educational system to educate people to have a sense of democratic coexistence. This requires not only reframing educational practices, but directly teaching human rights, the struggle against discrimination, the rejection of stereotypes, interculturalism and solidarity. The Basque Government requires the promotion of global school projects and the co-ordination of teaching staff with external resources.

Final reflections

There has been little analysis of the historical development of the concept of citizenship, apart from some recent contributions in this field. Our model of citizenship itself has developed, partly through the profound social, technological and economic changes that characterise contemporary society. Citizenship now emphasises participation, property, rights and responsibilities, extending the traditional liberal model elaborated by Marshall. Present problems include particular deficiencies in citizenship, from some lack of interest in exercising certain political rights to the difficulties of some groups who are deprived of the right to citizenship, such as some immigrants.

The challenge facing education is to assist in learning to know, to do, to coexist and to be – the four pillars of education established in the UNESCO Delors report (Delors, 1996). This is reflected in the project for a prepared, active, critical and responsible citizenry, who are confident to participate in public life (Eurydice, 2004; Council of Europe, 2001).

The social sciences teacher has a complex task: more competences are demanded of the teacher, while the material that pupils must cover becomes less precise – as is the case with citizenship education (Gómez, 2005). Challenges to the work of the teaching staff include:

- using new methods of education that lead to independent learning

- strengthening active methodologies that allow the development of critical thought

- developing values and local and global feelings of pupils

- coordinating with other departments or areas

- coordinating with other social agents

To achieve this, teachers will have to extend their professional tasks, which traditionally have focused only on academic aspects. They will need to recognise that success does not lie in implanting the subject, but in the conceptual and methodological aspects related to citizenship itself. Finally, in the education of citizens all educational agents must assume a shared responsibility.

Note

We are grateful to Ana Isabel López Arribas and Ana Basterra for their comments and the documentation they provided for this section.

8

People meet history – a Swedish television production in a medieval milieu

Lars Berggren and Roger Johansson

'Riket – The Kingdom': a reality series in a middle-ages milieu

During the autumn of 2004, Swedish Television broadcast a reality series called *Riket – The Kingdom*. This was set in a contrived medieval environment: to create a suitable atmosphere reminiscent of the Middle Ages for participants and audience, the series was filmed at the medieval Polish castle of Grodziec. The format was a reality show, in the last episode of which one of the participants was to win the much-desired master-jewel; the sub-text of the series was man's lust for power as driving force throughout history.

The series was a large and expensive project for Swedish Television (STV), with a budget of over three million euros and a production team of over a hundred people. The series combined three production methods: outside broadcasting, reality and drama, and used new technologies to improve sound and picture quality. It was introduced to the public through a massive and successful publicity campaign, with a series of popular events leading up to the series to increase expectations. Few television productions had received such national press coverage as *Riket*, consisting of interviews with the compère, actor Stefan Sauk and others responsible for the production.

At the beginning of the series in late November 2004, the first episode attracted almost 1.3 million viewers (14.9 %), but then sank to 8.4% in late December, rising again for the final broadcast to 1.2 million (14.1%). The average audience over the series was 12.3% of viewers. The closest comparison is to the reality series *Robinson*, set on an island in the South Seas in the present time. This series also had a number of contests with the aim of finding a winner. When *Robinson* was broadcast in 2003, the series had an average audience of 30.5%, and the final episode in February 2004 was watched by 38% of viewers. In comparison, *Riket* was not a success: as well as disappointing viewer figures, the project failed to attract a young school-age audience, one of its expressed aims.

Accompanying the television series, the *Riket* project included a web site and a history book. On the web site, viewers were able to follow the series, chat and express views about it, and also make links to books with historical references to the Middle Ages. These were intended to be used as teaching aids if teachers used the series as a starting point for history lessons in the classroom. The companion history book was a basic volume about the Middle Ages, written for generally interest and to be used as a textbook in schools.

The following summary, from STV's homepage after the first episode, provides a useful summary of the series as a whole:

> Sixteen former strangers meet. The hunt for the jewel, the role of Master and the achievement of power in *Riket* was clear from the series' first challenge. Each participant was tied to a pole. They were challenged to use their ingenuity to free themselves, run to the jewel and put it over their head. David was the first participant to free himself, and thus became the first Master. (http://svt.se/svt/jsp/Crosslink.jsp?d=23133)

The objective of the contest was made clear immediately: the winner of *Riket* was the one who got the jewel. By connecting power to the individual, any attempt to relate power to the collective, or to change the rules of the game so that singular interest was challenged by solidarity, was foiled from the outset. Societal structures cannot be changed. History was used to legitimate a particular view of mankind. The series also demonstrated the ways in which history can be used to look from our own point in time towards a horizon of new liberalism.

Before the series opened, the producer Ebba Kronkvist said 'The challenges confronting the participants are about power, class conflict and injustice. I think it's a good thing that we raise these issues; I am proud of that aspect of *Riket*' (*Svenska Dagbladet*, 2005). But the articles about the series on SVT's homepage and in the press were no different from those about any other reality television series. The focus on the competition and the personal intrigues involved in winning were central in the media coverage. There were even critical voices about some elements of the series that could be interpreted as bullying. There was also criticism from some Christian and Muslim leaders when a Muslim participant was required to crawl on his knees around a cross: critics said this was suggestive of the Inquisition. Others thought the ideology behind the series illustrated the current climate of neo-liberalism (see for example *Aftonbladet,* 2005; *Expressen,* 2005).

We would like in this chapter to discuss two interpretations of the series. The first concerns the series' pretensions to authenticity.

As indicated earlier, the introductions to the series gave the impression that one would meet the Middle Ages through *Riket*. For example, the series' homepage says:

> Two hundred castles and strongholds were explored throughout Europe in an effort to make everything as realistic as possible, so that the participants can mentally be transferred to the Middle Ages. (http://svt.se/svt/jsp/Crosslink.jsp?d=23166)

Another example is in the introduction to the book *Riket*:

> Many of us fantasise about what it would be like to live in another age, and now we've got the chance! In Swedish Television's bold

venture *Riket*, participants try out what it would be like to live in the fourteenth century, both as a rich person in a castle and as a peasant in a farmer's hovel. The milieu is as authentic as it can be – but how much do we really know about that time? (Wessnert, 2004)

On the series' homepage, Swedish Television says:

> The reality team portrays all that took place in the day to day life of the poor and the rich, and the conflicts that arose between them. (http://svt.se/svt/jsp/Crosslink.jsp?d=23166)

Reality is thus given quite a different meaning from the way in which historical research strives to reach and describe; to reflect an historical reality based on the historical context of the time. Now we move that reality to our own time, or rather to the presumed reality of the future.

By placing *Riket* in the Middle Ages, it could be said that the series is a response to the popular interest in Jan Guillou's series of novels about the character Arn. Fiction is interwoven with fact – and vice versa – in books, brochures and theme walks. (In a forthcoming licentiate thesis to be presented at Malmö University College, Carina Renander shows the importance of Guillou's series of novels in terms of the culture of history and historical consciousness).

The other perspective concerns what historians sometimes call grand narratives that place us in a longer time-frame in which we can begin to understand who we are. One such grand narrative is that of our own country. A survey of history books from secondary schools in the various countries from 1980, presented by a group of European history teachers at the International Congress of Historical Sciences in Oslo in 2000, showed that they had become increasingly nationalistic (*The teaching of history: new techniques, textbooks and the place of history in the curriculum*, 2000). More space in each book was being devoted to the individual country, despite current political ambitions to create a general European history. One can see the interest shown in the Swedish Middle Ages as a phase in the same process, where the focus is on building a nation. The *Riket* project can be seen as countering this: both programme and complementary material (internet sites and books) can be interpreted as part of the highly-charged conflict between a nationalist Swedish story and an attempt at forming a European identity. During the 1993 History Year, there was an intense discussion about a travelling exhibition on Swedish history which expressed a traditional view of Swedish national history. Critics held the underlying views of the exhibition to be nationalistic. From a European perspective, the television view of the Middle Ages might be interpreted as Euro-centric: the western view of the Middle Ages has centre stage (Rüsen, 2002).

Riket, the television series, can therefore be interpreted as a story about the European Middle Ages, independent of geographic location, in the same way as the Swedish school curriculum presumes the Christian tradition and Western humanism. In a sense, though it might be seen as far-fetched, one could identify a grand narrative about everyone throughout the world as being Europeans.

'Riket' at Malmö Museum

The television series was produced by Swedish Television in the city of Malmö. The city museum is in the 16th century castle of Malmöhus, and it tried to take advantage of the interest that *Riket* was expected to have for young people with an exhibition of the props used in the series. On 27 November 2004, the same day *Riket's* first episode was broadcast, the exhibition '*Riket*: glimpses of history' opened:

> *Riket* takes place in an historical milieu, where poor and rich alike battle for honour, glory and the magnificent Master Jewel ... What is play and what is for real, what is truth and what is fiction? (Malmö museer, 2004)

This is comparable to the series' homepage, where the same text is given, describing *Riket* as in some way medieval.

Through interactive exhibits, Malmö Museum has tried to build pedagogically on the presumed interest there would be in the Middle Ages, anticipating that young people would have developed this from the television series. The content of the series was used to make the museum exhibition accessible to school classes. The items displayed were in a sense real, and the pedagogics of the exhibition uses this to engage with children's thoughts about the series and discuss issues with them. It was planned that children would be able to discuss questions about the Middle Ages – people's lives and thoughts, then and now; whether the series really mirrors past reality; and, if so, whose reality. Thus the exhibition presents a pedagogy that aims to help teachers work with children's ideas and interpretation of a reality that is mirrored by a television drama.

A question needs to be raised: what responses would the exhibition provoke if the museum guides did not present their narratives and explanations? Is it possible that what is being presented is neither the SVT television series nor the Middle Ages, but a third narrative, created by Malmö Museum? The museum had real opportunities to explore the problems suggested by the series and its relationship to the Middle Ages, and of the Middle Ages as a concept.

The exhibition closed with an exciting seminar, with participants across Sweden. Many people attended and discussed the meaning of the series and the values and reality it mirrored. The seminar became an important part of the exhibition, and widened the discussion across different cultural institutions.

History at school and outside school
The authors of this chapter are both active historians working in – amongst other things – teacher education. Our analysis is from the perspective of historical/didactic research on people's confrontation with history, in this case particularly from the viewpoint of teacher education and the school system. Clearly both the television series and its complementary material and Malmö Museum's interpretation are different arenas in which history is being transferred and in which people are confronted with interpretations of history.

Current history/didactic research maintains that people meet history in many different areas of life, for example through the media, museums, computer games and fiction. These channels for transferring history are increasing, including a greater variety of television programmes. Swedes no longer meet one story through Swedish television but many, through the variety of programmes with historical themes. They vary from documentaries to reality series costumed as history, which in some cases can become exhibitions at museums such as the one for *Riket,* whose props and costumes were exhibited to the public.

This greater access to history is a challenge to the role of the school as the more traditional conveyor of history. This is not new, but many researchers have observed that the school's role is no longer as self-evident as in the past (Bryld, 1999; Jensen, 2003).

But it is broadly true that it is through the school that the state, through teaching history among other subjects, tries to instil in its citizens a consistent story of how our society developed, what it is like today and how it can be expected to be in the future. This entails a view of history that incorporates how we see ourselves and how society would like to present itself, often set in comparison with the wider world. There are a number of conflicting ideas in this, but the values of a society are prominent when those who take the initiative in problem formulation write curricula. It is increasingly clear that history has a role in wider societal debate, so it is not surprising that the subject of history has reached the realms of television's reality shows.

The Danish history-didactist Bernard Eric Jensen has suggested a model to illustrate how a person produces and reproduces historical consciousness. Jensen defines historical consciousness as the way humans interpret and understand the processes and connections between the past, the present and the future.

What Jensen is trying to show in this is that history is found all around us, in an array of forms and manifestations, that we are confronted by history by each of these simultaneously and school is one arena among many – but also that the writing of history is created around us, and universities and museums are only two among many fields for the writing of history, or the teaching of history. There are many who tell stories, and this is not extraordinary or surprising. People are confronted by, and constantly creating, history in their everyday lives.

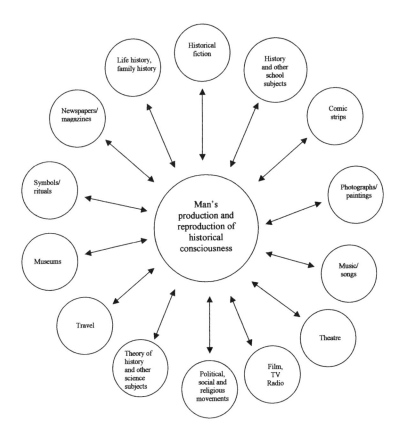

Based on: Bernard Eric Jensen, 2003, p 88.

Consider in what context *Riket* would have been viewed by students. They are forming ideas about history, developing their understanding of history and historical consciousness – how they write themselves into history. Using Jensen's diagram as a starting point, the question arises: what is it that students meet when they see *Riket*, or visit the exhibition?

How does the school interact with the outside world?

The world outside school has a great influence on one's concept of history: this can be empirically verified. For example, the American study by Roy Rosenzweig and David Thelen examined responses from 1,500 adult Americans between 1994 and 1995. This demon-

134

strated a massively negative impression of the teaching of history in school – 'It was a giant data dump', as one person put it. A chapter heading in the book sums the situation up: 'The sad story of history in schools' (Rosenzweig and Thelen, 1998, 109). This is not directly comparable to the situation in, for example, Sweden. A recently completed national evaluation of Swedish compulsory schooling shows that there is an extensive interest in the subject of history, and that pupils' attitudes to teaching of history is positive (Berggren and Johansson, 2005). But an obvious conclusion is that this teaching must include subject matter and be carried out in a way that pupils see as relevant and meaningful, and that they can use in the development of their own historical consciousness.

We suggest however that the conclusion can also be drawn that in Sweden people also perceive arenas other than school as important, relevant and meaningful in forming a consciousness of history. Rosenzweig and Thelen's results are thus of great interest. Their study asked respondents which of a list of activities they had pursued in the previous twelve months (see Table 1 on page 136).

People feel an affinity with their forebears, and photographs and museums not only inspire individual memories but also contribute to a collective perception of the past. Their study includes many descriptions of meetings people have had with the past.

An important task for any government is, and has always been, to transfer cultural heritage from one generation to another. This, above all, takes place in the education system. The 2000 curriculum for history in Sweden states that the subject contributes in developing 'a cultural identity from the cultural heritage passed from generation to generation'. But it is far from self-evident what this cultural heritage consists of. In a society that is increasingly characterised by ethnic and cultural multiplicity, the substance of our cultural heritage inevitably becomes more complex. This is important, especially as teaching in school is carried out in an institutionalised form largely using pre-prepared study materials and qualified teachers. Teaching in our schools forms part of a greater institutionalised structure, where goals and forms of education are regulated by government

Table 1: Percentage of Americans surveyed who have in the past 12 months:

	Percent
Looked at photographs with family or friends	91
Taken photographs or videos to preserve memories	83
Watched any movies or television programmes about the past	81
Attended a family reunion or a reunion of some other group of people with whom you have a shared experience	64
Visited any history museums or historic sites	57
Read any books about the past	53
Participated in any hobbies or worked on any collections related to the past	39
Looked into the history of your family or worked on your family tree	36
Written in a journal or diary	29
Participated in a group devoted to studying, preserving, or presenting the pas	20

Source: Rosenzweig and Thelen, 1998, p19

and Parliament and evaluated by national authorities such as the National Agency for Education.

Some central concepts

Cultural heritage is a concept that attempts to describe the people's relationship to the culture in which they live. This can be problematised in a number of ways. In an anthropological frame, or from a constructivist concept of culture, everybody has a relationship with the culture or the surroundings in which they live. Consequently, nobody is without culture: we have all come into contact with, distanced ourselves from, assumed and become participants in some form of culture ('Cultural heritage', in *GADs historieleksikon*, 2003).

In everyday use, the concept has also assumed another meaning, referring to a common cultural frame of reference – for example, a Swedish, European or humanist cultural heritage. In this interpretation, cultural heritage has assumed a normative meaning that implies a consensus as to what cultural values and knowledge should be transferred to the next generation.

In this latter interpretation, the concept has implications for how our teaching of history should be formed and what historical knowledge should be given to students. Thus the teaching of history becomes a way of creating a collective cultural identity in the next generation. If we allow the concept of cultural heritage to assume this normative meaning, it is not surprising that public discussion of what our cultural heritage should contain leads to heated, and sometimes irreconcilable, attitudes and feelings.

Memory and identity is a second concept that requires discussion. Maurice Halbwachs suggests that collective memory is socially constructed (Halbwachs, 1992). Individuals remember, but draw on a specific context when recreating the past. Therefore the frame of reference, including cultural heritage, is profoundly important when we refer to collective memories. These references may differ between social groups and classes, associations and families. Memory and identity are concepts that may connect to thoughts and images about history. When people construct their identities they refer to 'the other': forming an identity constructs the self in relationship to others. Memory is activated and loaded with meaning when it connects with narratives on the individual and the collective level. Some examples of how memory might be referred to a common frame of references will illustrate this.

Some examples

The department store of Tati in Paris made use of a well-known painting in its advertisements. People were obviously expected to know the famous painting by Eugene Delacroix, *La Liberté guidant le peuple*, of the revolution of 1830. The original painting showed the revolution as a drama: an alliance of students, workers and the bourgeoisie rush forward, led by Marianne with the tricolour in her hands. Every French citizen recognises this painting. However, in Tati´s version the context was different: people are rushing to the store's sales to get there first. Instead of a gun in his hands, the young student has a cell phone; instead of a rifle, the revolutionary bourgeois holds an umbrella in the store's colours. Marianne with the tricolour is replaced by a young woman holding the Tati flag.

A second example is from the entrance of a restaurant in Nuuk in Greenland. A poster shows a picture of an 18th century well-to-do woman with a Danish text: 'Welcome to the dining-house of Gertrud Rask'. For the advertisement to work, one is expected to have some knowledge of what the painting expresses, and the frame of reference is probably only relevant to those who have been to Greenland.

Gertrud Rask was the wife of the Norwegian missionary Hans Egede, who is said to have christened the Inuit people, and also to have been the founder of the Danish colony. In this narrative, his wife Gertrud Rask becomes the godmother of Greenland – and who would not want to be served dinner in her kitchen?

These are the associations people are supposed to derive from the poster: the precondition is that one must have some knowledge about the wife of Hans Egede and the story behind her. At a deeper level, this is part of the colonial narrative, in which the mother from the Nordic countries supposedly includes the Greenlandic population within her family.

Memory takes on a more serious meaning in French postcards from the beginning of World War One. They refer to not only the memory of the war, but are also a personal testimony of war. We often don't know the conclusion: we only know that the postcards had senders and receivers. When such postcards were sent, they had a specific meaning to inspire and mobilise the population against the enemy, creating patriotic and nationalistic sentiments. Sometimes this was done by referring to the war between France and Germany in 1870.

There is a well-known photograph of King Gustav V of Sweden and the social democratic leader Hjalmar Branting taken at the beginning of the 20th century that has been widely used in picture books and school history text books. The gentlemen seem to be talking to each other confidentially, though the politician has respectfully taken off his hat. This photograph has a serious meaning, because the picture also tells a story of how Swedish society would like to describe itself. The picture is not only part of the narrative about these leading figures from the past; it is also a narrative that has political and ideological meaning. It might be interpreted as a scene showing hegemony, but it could also be interpreted as showing class collaboration and, in this way, it becomes a statement about basic conditions within Swedish society today. The photograph naturally provokes the question of what it is we want to re-create or what it is we want someone to remember.

The examples show how actors use paintings, postcards or photographs for different ideological, political, commercial and other purposes (on different uses of history, see Karlsson 1999, p57). At the same time, they are interpreted by humans in activating historical memory to construct identities and expectations. From these examples, we might ask what kind of identities and memories the television series *Riket* activated, and which uses of history the producers employed.

History and the Swedish compulsory school

The current school history curriculum, written in 2000, underlines various meanings of the concept of history. It refers to an intercultural perspective, to cultural identity and to a cultural heritage: 'The subject contributes to developing not only an inter-cultural perspective, but also cultural identity on the basis of cultural heritage, which is transferred from generation to generation.' (http://www3.skol verket.se/ki/eng/comp, p66). Culture is found under the heading 'Goals to strive towards', where it is connected to other structural concepts such as identity and historical consciousness. One goal is for pupils to 'acquire a sense of history, which makes easier the interpretation of current events and developments, and creates preparedness for the future' (*ibid*).

The curriculum does not define any further in what sense these various concepts are to be used. 'Goals to strive towards' also asks that pupils should be able to identify processes of development and change, gain knowledge of important figures and events as well as the ability to critically assess and interpret various sources and references.

The curriculum lists goals that pupils should have attained by the end of their ninth year of schooling:

Pupils should:

- be able to present important events and be familiar with the personalities, ideas and changes in the historical developments in Sweden, the Nordic area and Europe, as well as be able to make comparisons with other countries

- be familiar with historical developments in some of the world's leading powers during different periods

- have an insight into how major social upheavals have altered people's living conditions

- be able to identify and reflect on some of the different historical events and developments of significance for our own age

- be aware of and able to give examples of historical events and conditions that can be looked at from different points of view

- be able to reflect over how information and propaganda have been used before and are used today as a means of exerting influence (http://www3.skolverket.se/ki/eng/comp)

How is a television series like *Riket* and its complementary materials used in teaching in schools? Arguments by Jensen and the American study, among others, lead to the conclusion that pupils come into contact with history in many different arenas. It is therefore important to connect with, work through, problemetise and discuss the interpretations of history that are portrayed in television, computer games, comics, films and the like. It is essential that teachers use the opportunities presented to them in series and stories of, for example, the Middle Ages, and this applies to *Riket* as well as books about *Arn*. But how? What questions should be asked? How should we work through and problemetise *Riket*?

Riket attempts to teach history. On the homepage 'Tell a Friend' section, *Riket* is described as 'an exciting power play set in days of old. In a time-faithful milieu, peasants challenge the rich in a battle for honour, glory and riches'. The evening paper *Aftonbladet's* interview with the producers in December 2004: 'We have been inspired by the historical epoch of the Middle Ages and tried to create an exciting duel using that as a starting point' (*Aftonbladet,* 2004).

Which perspective comes to the fore? Where is the gender perspective? What are the fields of cooperation and conflict in medieval society? Even when there is a revolution in the television programme, the rules of the series are hardly broken. The poor do not build a collective opposition and depose the game leader Stefan Sauk. He has not attained power by the grace of God, but by that of the producers of Swedish television, and that is where the limit of revolution is drawn. Medieval society is shown through current perspectives such as power, exclusion and individualism in a neo-liberal rendering.

> What is the role of an object in an historical story? What happens when a museum exhibits props from a television series? What is it that is being exhibited? – Swedish TV's programme series, or the Middle Ages? Can interest be stimulated in both? What pedagogical possibilities does this collaboration give rise to? How is a museum prepared for meeting a new view of history?

These reflections come from one of our courses for prospective teachers of history at Malmö University (though it is not about medieval history). In the initial course of the main subject, History and Learning, our students begin by undertaking a 15 ECTS points unit called 'Sweden's Twentieth Centuries' – in the plural – in which assessment is an essay based on a deep interview with an older relative, whose own experiences of twentieth century history are contrasted with the materials in textbooks and museums. This gives our students three insights:

Firstly, that there are many interpretations of history. Facts are always contained in a frame of interpretation, which itself is based on certain assumptions. Through problemetising these academic and non-academic assumptions, students are given the chance to problemetise representations of history.

Secondly, that one meets history in two ways: genetically from then to now, and genealogically, from now to then. By connecting both functions, a greater understanding of historical events and contexts is achieved.

Thirdly, it is people of flesh and blood who have borne history. By following historical subjects closely, one is also able to work through peoples' existential need to develop their historical consciousness. How the interpretation of the past, the understanding of the present and the expectations of the future connect together in a dynamic process – all of this is an important lesson to learn.

Riket creates an historical backdrop to tell something. The question is what? Is *Riket* primarily about the Middle Ages, or about people of today, about class relations or about the way society might look in the future? By using *Riket* as a springboard for the teaching of history, by working through and problemetising the messages and scenarios in a medieval costume drama, we can help our pupils to develop their historical consciousness.

Note

This article is an abridged version of an article by Roger Johansson, published in A.Högberg and H. Kihlström (eds), *Medeltid på tevetid – en dokusåpas historiedidaktik* (2005).

9

Leading Forward: The experiences of Palestinians and Israelis in the Learning Each Other's Historical Narratives Project

Sami Adwan and Dan Bar-On

Background and Introduction

Despite its limitations and weaknesses, the Oslo Accord of 1993 was an important event in the history of Palestinian and Israeli conflict and reconciliation. A top-down decision-making approach to resolve the conflict, it was the first peace agreement signed by leaders of both sides, creating hopes of a better future. Most Palestinians received it with joy, happiness and great expectations: people of all ages went on the streets singing, dancing with olive branches and giving sweets to the Israeli soldiers that were to leave their cities.

The Accord allowed many Israeli and Palestinian peace organisations to be established that worked jointly and separately at grassroots level in a bottom-up approach to mitigate the consequences of the conflict. The period from 1993 to 2000 has been seen by many as a major era of peace: it witnessed hundreds of people-to-people projects involving thousands of Palestinians and Israelis. But it also witnessed stagnation of the peace process at the political level. The bottom-up and the top-down approaches were not well synchronised, and this helps explain the failure of the peace process and the dying away of the Oslo Accord.

This chapter describes some of the continuing educational work of one such bottom-up group, the Peace Research Institute in the Middle East (PRIME). PRIME is a joint Palestinian and Israeli non-governmental and non-profit organisation that was established in 1998. The process of development and the principles that under-pinned PRIME are outlined in the box below.

Box 9.1: PRIME: a Palestinian-Israeli Peace Research Institute

The Peace Research Institute in the Middle East (PRIME) is a joint Palestinian and Israeli non-governmental and non-profit organisation established in 1998. A group of Palestinian and Israeli intellectuals, with the help of the Peace Research Institute in Frankfurt, decided to build understanding, trust and tolerance between their peoples through cooperation based on equality at all levels and in all processes: thinking, planning, implementation and evaluation. Many of the founders of PRIME had been involved in forms of cooperation at the personal level, but they now sought to formalise and institutionalise this: PRIME's main purpose was to pursue coexistence and peace-building through joint research and outreach activities.

PRIME's offices are located in Talitha Kumi School/Beit Jala for several reasons: it is a locality that both Israelis and Palestinians can reach freely, it has facilities in the school that include meeting rooms, dining and residential accommodation, and it had the full support of the then school Principal, Wilhelm Goller. PRIME continues to be supported by the new school principal, Dr Georg Duerr. The school is now seen as an oasis of peace, open to all kinds of peace-building projects. The staff and directors believe in ending the conflict peacefully, and seek a bi-national peace accord, supported by the international community, to end all forms of conflict and to establish an independent Palestinian State with East Jerusalem its capital, within the 1967 borders, living alongside a secure Israeli State.

PRIME seeks to reduce the asymmetrical relationship between Israelis and Palestinians. Within the Institute there is complete parity, symmetry and equality between the two sides. The Institute promotes human rights, full academic freedom and independence from political interest. It demonstrates practical solidarity when these principles are violated or threatened. It strives for scholarly excellence.

The Institute aims to

- build an intellectual infrastructure for peace
- influence the public agenda in Israel and Palestine
- suggest proposals to overcome obstacles to peace-building
- analyse long-term regional issues
- develop a generation of leaders committed to peaceful co-existence and cooperation
- contribute to the strengthening of civil society
- serve as a reference centre for cooperative activities
- encourage joint academic activities between members

The strength of the Institute's commitment is shown by the way in which its programmes continue through the political and military tension that periodically interrupts the peace process. It is led in a way that reflects its dedication to parity in all activities: it is led by two presidents, two directors and a joint executive and general committee. English is the agreed language of PRIME, used in meetings, reporting and documentation.

Since 1998 the Institute has organised joint research projects, meetings, workshops and conferences in which equal numbers of Israeli and Palestinian schoolteachers, students, professors and other experts, with international participants, have worked together. All meetings took place in the region: participants were able to share residential accommodation, to socialise with each other and to share personal and professional stories.

Strong friendships and relationships have grown between the two sides: individual commitment to PRIME's mission and objectives has increased, and involvement in PRIME's projects has enhanced particpants' hopes and belief in peace and a better future.

The outbreak of the Palestinian *Al-Aqsa Intifada* (the Second Intifada) in October 2000 became a turning-point in the history of PRIME and its activities. The situation between Israelis and Palestinian deteriorated to the extent that meetings between the two sides became dangerous and almost impossible. Many Palestinians found it hard to see the value of cooperating when the Palestinian National Authority Territories (the Occupied Territories) were under siege, when these areas were reoccupied through short and long-term incursions, when hundreds of Israeli military checkpoints and barriers had been established which limited Palestinian movement, when Palestinians' homes were being destroyed and trees uprooted, and when there were killings and assassinations. From the Israeli perspective, attacks on them by Palestinians created a sense of fear and insecurity. This strengthened right-wing parties, and later led to the *Likud* party winning political power.

The staff of PRIME discussed the possibilities of continuing to work under these extremely difficult conditions, and decided to cooperate as much as possible. This was not easy: plans and programmes had to be modified to emphasise processes rather than outcomes, much time and energy had to be given to finding accessible places to meet and to obtaining permits for the Palestinian members to attend, and it was necessary to avoid too much public and media attention. Our expectations became long-term, rather than immediate. It became much simpler to organise meetings outside the region.

It was equally difficult for the two directors of PRIME to meet in the first year of the *Intifada*. Face-to-face meetings were difficult: cooperation was more frequently maintained by telephone and e-mail contacts. Many meetings were at checkpoints, to exchange materials, offer mutual support, and to have brief discussions on projects.

Many Palestinian and Israeli joint organisations and activities ended: hundreds of cooperative projects stopped, and others were postponed until the situation improved. PRIME was one of the few organisations that decided to continue, taking on the frustration, hopelessness and helplessness but also the possibility of moving towards peace and justice through its projects.

What were these projects? Two major projects were continued. One focused on oral history accounts from members of both societies. The aim is to develop a database record of the conflict by documenting family stories through videotaped interviews, to create an oral museum. Hundreds of 1948 Palestinian refugees and Israeli Jewish immigrants have been interviewed, and three films have been produced: *Haifa in the Memory, The Silenced Voices of Haifa and Beit Jubreen – Revadim 1948-2005: Palestinian Refugees and Israeli Jewish listening to each other's stories*. (Beit Jubreen is a Palestinian town, now within Israel: its Palestinian inhabitants were expelled in 1948 and now live in the Al-Azah and Al-Dehaishah refugee camps in Bethlehem district. Revadim is an Israeli kibbutz built there after Beit Jubreen had been destroyed in 1948.)

The second project, 'Learning each other's historical narratives: Palestinians and Israelis', is the major focus of this chapter.

Learning one another's histories

In this project, twelve Palestinian and Israeli history school teachers worked together under the guidance and supervision of two historians, Professor Eyal Naveh from Tel Aviv University and Professor Adnan Massallam from Bethlehem University. The objectives of the project were to:

- teach school pupils, Palestinian and Israeli, about each others' historical narratives

- train Palestinians and Israeli teachers how to teach both narratives to their pupils

- develop a teacher's guide

The project does not yet aim at criticising or changing the different historical narratives, nor does it seek to create a joint or bridging narrative. It simply brings to the attention of both sides that another narrative exists as well as their own. They should learn to respect and understand the narrative of the other side even if they do not fully agree with all its contents.

When schoolchildren study history in times of war or conflict, they generally learn only their side of the story, which is naturally considered to be the right version. History teaching can often be doctrinaire, taught to justify our side and presenting a negative view of the other. Very often, one side's hero becomes the other side's monster. Many research studies (for example, the long-running series conducted by the Georg Eckert Institute of International Textbook Research in Braunschweig) show how school textbooks usually focus on conflict between groups, and the human losses and suffering, in the process neglecting periods of peace or coexistence between the two sides. Teachers are put in the position of being cultural emissaries of the nation: they are expected to emphasise the goodness of their country's side and the evil of the other country. Teachers are trained to teach their own narrative, to defend and to legitimise it and to make sure their pupils accept it.

School textbooks generally deny the existence of any narrative other than their country's own account. If other accounts are presented, it is with the objective of demonstrating the wrong-headedness of the other and of proving the justification of their country's position. Ruth Firer from the Hebrew University and Sami Adwan (one of the authors of this chapter) have analysed how the Israeli-Palestinian conflict has been presented in the history and civic schoolbooks of both nations. One of their major findings was that both school textbooks include only their own narrative (Adwan and Firer, 1997, 1999; Firer and Adwan, 2004).

Neglecting or denying the existence of the narrative of the other contributes to the maintenance of enmity, hatred and negative stereotypes. This in turn sustains the conflict and makes achieving a peaceful solution more difficult. Knowing the other side's narrative should help mitigate the conflict, create empathy and therefore open possibilities for openness and compromise.

Teachers are the main protagonists in teaching: they have enormous influence in forming the attitudes, values and norms of their pupils. They are therefore the most important potential agents of change. Their role is critical if there is to be any change or development in education and its role in building peace. We therefore focused on the role that teachers would be expected to play in the project. They were to be asked to write the historical narratives with which the pupils would work. This would help them develop a sense of ownership, ensure their commitment to the process, and demonstrate their achievement through the product. They would be able to develop their writing skills and their teaching approaches in handling classroom approaches with the narratives from the two sides. It would be a professional development programme, as well as a curriculum project.

Teachers were recruited from the two communities in separate processes. Each side selected six history teachers, three male, three female, chosen from different types of schools. The selection was of teachers of grades nine and ten. Their command of English was an important criterion for their selection, as was their willingness, commitment and motivation to work with members of the other community.

Pupils in grades nine and ten (aged between 15 and 16) from different schools were chosen to study the different narratives, because they had already studied some history and would be able to develop their own approaches to learning. Two years after this age, they would be expected to go to university, or to work in the case of the Palestinians, or army service in the case of the Israelis.

Our work with the teachers was in English. This gave some teachers some difficulties, so when necessary there was some sporadic translation into Arabic or Hebrew. The Israeli narratives were first written in Hebrew, and the Palestinian narratives in Arabic: both sets of narratives were then translated into the other language, and then into English.

Working together

Most of the meetings with the teachers were for two days: the exceptions were two meetings held in Turkey and Germany, each a week long. Some of the two-day meetings were held in Jerusalem, organised at roughly three-monthly intervals, dependent largely on

149

when the Palestinian team could obtain permits to enter the city. The other meetings were held in Talitha Kumi school in Beit Jala: one Israeli teacher was not able to join these meetings, for security reasons.

The first meeting started with a long opening session in which the teachers got to know one another. They introduced themselves, explained the meaning of their names, talked about the most important events in their lives, and described their professional and academic backgrounds. Subsequent meetings always began with a similar long opening session, in which the teachers shared personal, social and professional stories and talked about what had happened to them since the last meeting. Fourteen of these meetings took place between January 2001 and December 2004.

The teachers worked in both single-nation and bi-national groups throughout the project. Small, bi-national groups worked on specific aspects, and were asked to report back to the whole group on their discussions, progress and difficulties encountered about the main issues. Sometimes local and international experts were invited to give lectures or to run simulations with the teachers. Meetings always ended with a session planning the next steps, and the programmes, dates and venues for the following meeting.

In their first meeting, the teachers were divided into three mixed groups of four, two members from each community. Each group was asked to select what they felt were the most significant events in their history: each group chose between ten and twelve events. They were then asked to explain why these events were so important, and to rate them all in order of importance.

Each group had to choose one event on which to start work. One group selected the Balfour Declaration, the second the 1948 war and the third the 1987 *Intifada*. In each group, each pair started to write their narrative of the event: they met the pair from the other community in their group, who would be working in parallel narrating the same event. They would discuss, explain and answer each others' questions. Following this, the two narratives would be translated into the other language and the teachers were able to read the other pair's narrative in their own language, and to comment on it.

The three pairs of narratives of the three events were published in the first booklet, side by side – with an empty space between them where the pupils could record their reactions. The teachers then used these narratives with their ninth and tenth-grade pupils. The first booklet was translated into English, French, Italian and Spanish, and these have been used in some schools in France and Italy.

The teams of teachers followed this with work, carried out through similar processes, on a second set of events and periods: the 1920s, the 1930s and the 1967 war. A second booklet based on these was published in Arabic and Hebrew in July 2005. The teams are now working on the dual narratives about the 1950s, the 1970s and the 1990s. These are to be published in the third booklet. All three booklets will be assembled in a single volume after some editing to ensure coverage of the main historical narratives of the 20th century. The final sequence will be from the Balfour Declaration, through the 1920s, the 1930s, the 1948 war, the 1950s, the 1967 war, the 1970s, the 1987 Palestinian *Intifada* and finally the 1990s.

Rules
In order to continue the dynamic of the processes and to avoid any unnecessary dispute or conflict, the group developed a set of rules and regulations.

Procedural rules
1. Do not interrupt anyone from talking for as long as s/he wishes

2. Do not criticise or deny a narrative from the other side

3. Do not ask or put pressure to people to change the other's narrative

4. Avoid using insensitive terms or difficult body language

5. Questions should ask for explanations of dates, events or people

6. Everyone must attend the full meetings punctually

Rules about the content

1. Information should be at a level suitable for the pupils

2. The language used in the narrative should be suitable for the pupils

3. Each narrative should be no more than twenty pages, including maps and illustrations

4. Each narrative should include a glossary that defines terms, places and individuals

5. Narratives should be followed by questions or dilemmas, so that pupils are asked to think and to develop opinions

6. All information that is quoted should be documented and referenced

Teachers' experiences and pupils' reactions

A few of the teachers in the project were unable to continue because of various political, logistical and psychological factors. One of the Palestinian teachers died in August 2002, during the project's first year (Yousuf Tumaizig had been arrested and jailed in Israeli prisons on more than twenty occasions). Another teacher, a member of the project from its inception, said at one point: 'I do not know who I am. From one part, I am here meeting with Israeli teachers and we are trying to understand each other, but only two hours ago I was humiliated at an Israeli military checkpoint.' An Israeli teacher commented, 'I do not feel safe coming to these meetings while my family is worrying'. Yet the commitment of the majority of the teachers increased and deepened through the project. One Israeli teacher said, 'This project is the only thing in the last two years that has given me hope'. A Palestinian teacher remarked, 'This project makes me better understand myself and the others'. The teachers developed personal and professional relationships among themselves.

The reaction of the pupils varied. Some pupils made comments such as:

> It is nice to know the narrative of those on the other side.
>
> Our narrative differs from theirs.
>
> I wonder how they react to our narrative?
>
> Even if there are differences, there are also some similarities in the narratives.
>
> Do their teachers teach our narrative? Can we trust them to do this?

Rather different examples of the pupils' reactions were remarks such as:

> Our narratives are fact but theirs are propaganda.
>
> It is good to know their narrative but still ours is the true one.
>
> They try to twist the reality and the history.
>
> Now I know why the conflict is so difficult to resolve.

The experience of the teachers was unique. They were introducing the narratives of the other side during the most difficult times of the conflict. Most teachers had to make special arrangements in order to introduce the booklet into their classrooms. Tactics employed included dividing their classes into small groups, teaching in the afternoon, teaching in teachers' homes, and teaching from the booklet in parts. Some of the teachers made comments such as 'It was a very enriching experience, but it was difficult'. The teachers reported that their pupils asked questions such as:

> Do you believe in their narratives?
>
> If you do not, why are you teaching us these narratives?
>
> Why are you teaching us their narrative at this time?
>
> Is it part of the normalisation processes?

Parents' reactions also reflected the tense political situation. Whilst some parents welcomed the initiative, others said it was not yet the time to teach these narratives to their children.

When they came to work on the second booklet, it was noticeable that teachers from both communities had become more sensitive to the other side's concerns and needs, but they were nevertheless able to maintain the essential elements of their own narratives. They were more willing to listen to the other side's point of view, and were able to avoid using hurtful and damaging language. They began to help each other in the selection of materials to add to their narratives, and offered resources for quotation and documentation. It was clear that they were more willing to allow more than one definition for certain terms: for example, the Palestinians ran away/were expelled in 1948. They were able to take note of advice and suggestions made by teachers from the other community about particular events and people. They could explain why particular elements were included, or not, in their narratives.

It was agreed that the language and the level of information in the second booklet were more suitable for the ninth and tenth grades pupils. It was only at the thirteenth meeting, in Germany, that one teacher asked the teachers of the other community: 'When I will teach the 1950s from your perspective, what would you like me to emphasise?' At the same time, the teachers were continuing to dispute the contents of particular events, issues such as the length of the narratives and the questions about detailed and visual descriptions of painful events.

The project attracted international media attention. Descriptions of the project were given in many newspapers, journals, and radio and television broadcasts. The booklet became one of the bestseller books in France for a few weeks in the summer of 2004. Locally, we tried to avoid too much exposure in the media, so as not to harm the dynamic of the process that had developed between the teachers. The Ministries and officials were generally less interested in the project, although on the Israeli side there was an attempt to stop it.

PRIME's co-directors, historians and teachers were invited to workshops in Italy, France, Croatia, Spain, the USA and Germany to present the project and describe the experiences and the challenges we had faced. Many scholars, teachers and researchers requested the first booklet, either to use in their own classes or as a basis for research. Many made comments, such as asking why we presented two separate narratives, and why did we not write a single bridging narrative?

Our response was that we support a two-State solution and, at this historical and political point in the conflict, both sides needed to first develop and present their own narrative separately, in order to feel safe and to give the other side the opportunity to respect it. This was the first time that both sides had been exposed to the narrative of the other in such a comprehensive way: time was needed to look again at their own narratives and to reflect. We were leaving the construction of bridging narratives to the individual and to the two communities in the future. It was our belief that these booklets, and the experience we had gained so far, would be valuable after a comprehensive peace agreement that ended the conflict.

One member of UNESCO staff commented on the booklet: 'This is an excellent example of learning the other side's history, that [has] never done before in this style'. A prominent developmental psychologist commented: 'Children have the capacity of containing more than one narrative from early on. Usually, we as adults lose some of that capacity later on.'

Finally, we do not claim that either the Israeli or the Palestinian narratives represent all Israelis or all Palestinians. Our feeling is that they represent about two-thirds of each population. It is clear that there are other, less comprehensive and compatible narratives in both societies that have not been represented in this project.

Our future plans

PRIME now plans to organise an international conference to present the project, the experience and the recommendations. We also plan a teacher's guide, which will summarise the teachers' experience and explain how to use and teach the books.

The Palestinian and Israeli teachers will train more teachers in the development and use of this approach. The Institute's staff is willing to train teachers from other countries about this new approach.

PRIME is willing to make this experience available to other organisations, schools and universities. The staff are willing to be part of a joint Israeli/Palestinian education committee in the future. When it is feasible, they would like to help train teachers and revise and improve current textbooks so that they become agents for peace-building. In addition, PRIME will conduct evaluation research to examine some of the important aspects of the two-narrative approach.

Lessons and challenges

It is not easy to be involved in a peace-building project when the conflict is wide-open and bloody; this is very stressful work. Those involved could easily lose their motivation and the hope, energy and vision needed to continue. Our experience suggests that leaders of projects in similar circumstances need to create activities that keep re-energising and re-motivating the team to continue to commit to the project. We needed the flexibility and willingness to adjust our plans and procedures when they did not work at particular points: for example, when we were working on the teachers' guide, the differences in method became too stressful for the two groups, so we delayed this and continued with writing narratives.

The progress of projects such as these is never linear. The first step does not always lead to the next. Sometimes we had to go back some steps before moving forward again. We found it critical always to build on what we had achieved, however little this was, and to focus on the processes rather than on the results. While our expectations were very clear, they were also modest. Rather than always thinking of what we hoped to achieve, we instead gave much thought to how we could continue the dynamic of the processes we had succeeded in developing. The psychological feelings of our team were very important, particularly negative emotions of fear and stress: the reality of daily suffering and violence affected the participants much more than our talking and meetings. As leaders of the project, we felt that we had to act in a sincere and honest manner, setting a model of co-operation for the group members.

People involved in projects such as this need to take care not to isolate themselves from their own communities: we would advise that they try to share their experiences with people around them who can offer support. It is rather easy for participants in such projects to be isolated. Whilst it is good to receive official support and endorsement, this cannot be counted on but at the same time it is important not to antagonise or confront authorities. People at the decision-making level may be able, as individuals, to offer support, but not feel able to do so as officials: this support may take much longer to be arrived at than might be anticipated.

The role of the media is paradoxical. It might help publicise the project and create support, appreciation and a sense of achievement. It can be supportive to know that others recognise the devotion, work and burden taken on by the participants in the project. There can be advice and suggestions, even words of sympathy and encouragement. This can help the project's funding, showing supporters where their money goes, and may even bring in further funding.

But media interest can also have serious negative impacts. The team might be accused of betraying their own community and of breaking faith with them, or be branded naive and unprofessional. Those working on the project might be charged with selfishness or self-interest. Media reports presented without the contextual framework of the project tend to emphasise weaknesses, damaging the project and prompting members of the team to leave. The team and the project become easy targets for those who have different viewpoints.

In conclusion, our experiences suggest that those participating in projects similar to ours may face all or some of a number of challenges:

- problems around language, particularly when mother tongues cannot be used equally by both sides

- asymmetry between the parties. One party has much more power than the other, and there will be unequal access to information and resources. The level of development of the two sides may be uneven

- cultural differences – customs, habits, values, the sense of time, gender issues – will differ. As an example, one group might be much more reticent in confronting the other group when this is needed

■ the pain of daily reality and the ability to adjust between hopes and fears

■ pressures and criticism from families, colleagues and friends

■ fear of failing, particularly as tangible results take a long time to emerge

■ logistical and financial difficulties, including funding, finding meeting places, dealing with the difficulties of permits and travelling difficulties

■ suspicion between the two sides, and questioning the truthfulness of the other

■ fear that the information being shared might be used for other, harmful, purposes

These projects were funded by a Wye River Grant, through the United States Embassy in Tel Aviv, the United States Consulate in East Jerusalem, the Ford Foundation and the Georg Eckert Institute in Braunschweig, Germany. The Georg Eckert Institute was established in the 1950s to analyse German, French and Polish school books: it supported the project meeting held in August 2004.

Appendix

Two Narratives of the Balfour Declaration
(the student version has empty space between the narratives for student reactions)

The Israeli Narrative: From the Balfour Declaration to the first White Paper
Zionism, the Jewish national movement, was born in the 19th century when the ideology embodied in the Enlightenment was disseminated in the European Jewish community. These new ideas planted the first seeds of Jewish nationalism; the subsequent birth of Zionism was the result of several factors:

1. The rise of modern anti-Semitism – a deeply-rooted and complicated mixture of traditional religious hatred augmented by 'scientific' racism which categorized Jews as a depraved and pernicious race.

2. The disappointment of western European Jews with the emancipation which pledged that the position of Jews in society would equal that of the Christians. The Jews were discouraged when it became clear that in many instances there was equality in name only. Discrimination continued.

3. New European nationalist movements such as those appearing in Italy and Germany inspired similar aspirations among the Jews.

4. An important element was the longing for Zion, an integral aspect of Jewish religious and national identity throughout history. This longing stemmed from the biblical promise that the land of Israel was given to the people of Israel by the God of Israel, and from memories of those historical eras when the people of Israel lived independently in their land. This concept inspired the national anthem, written at that time:

Hatikvah: The Hope

As long as in our heart of hearts
the Jewish spirit remains strong,
And we faithfully look toward the east,
Our eyes will turn to Zion.
We have not yet lost our hope,
The hope of two thousand years,
To be a free people in our land –
The land of Zion and Jerusalem.

The Zionist movement was born in the major centres of Jewish population in Europe, and its purpose was to return the Jewish people to its land and put an end to its abnormal situation among the nations of the world. At first there was a spontaneous emergence of local associations ('Lovers of Zion') out of which an organized political movement was established, thanks to the activities of 'The Father of Zionism,' Theodore Herzl [whose Hebrew name is Benjamin Ze'ev Herzl].

In 1882 there was a small wave of immigration [*aliya/aliyot*] to 'the land' [i.e. the land of Israel], the first of several. The purpose of these *aliyot* was not just to fulfil the religious obligations connected to the land, as had been the case in the past, but rather to create a new kind of Jew, a productive labourer who would work on his own land and help Zionism establish a Jewish political entity in the land of Israel.

There were two basic approaches to Zionism:

- practical Zionism focused on increasing immigration, purchasing land, and settling Jews on the land. By 1914, in the first two waves of immigration, nearly 100,000 people immigrated (although most of them later left the country). Dozens of agricultural settlements were established and there was a significant increase in the urban Jewish population

- political Zionism focused on diplomatic efforts to get support for Zionism from the great empires in order to obtain a legal and official charter for wide-scale settlement in the land

Chaim Weizmann, who became Zionism's leader after Herzl's death, integrated both aspects of the movement.

[The original version shows a picture of the Moshav Nahalal, a semi-cooperative agricultural settlement established in the Jezreel Valley in 1921.]

The Balfour Declaration

The first time any country expressed support for Zionism was in a letter sent by Lord Balfour, Minister of Foreign Affairs, to Lord Rothschild, a leader of the Jewish community in Great Britain. It came to be known as the Balfour Declaration. The letter was dated November 2, 1917, shortly before the end of World War I. It expressed the support of the British Government for establishing a national home for the Jewish people in the land of Israel:

Foreign Office
November 2nd, 1917

Dear Lord Rothschild,

I have much pleasure in conveying to you, on behalf of His Majesty's Government, the following declaration of sympathy with Jewish Zionist aspirations which has been submitted to, and approved by, the Cabinet.

'His Majesty's Government view with favour the establishment in Palestine of a national home for the Jewish people, and will use their best endeavours to facilitate the achievement of this object, it being clearly understood that nothing shall be done which may prejudice the civil and religious rights of existing non-Jewish communities in Palestine, or the rights and political status enjoyed by Jews in any other country.'

I should be grateful if you would bring this declaration to the knowledge of the Zionist Federation.

Yours sincerely,

Arthur James Balfour

161

The Palestinian Narrative: The Balfour Declaration

Historical background

In April 1799, Napoleon Bonaparte put forth a plan for a Jewish state in Palestine. During the siege of Acre, he sought to enlist Jewish support in return for which he promised to build the Temple. The project failed after the defeat of Napoleon in the battles of Acre and Abu-Qir. It represents the first post-Renaissance expression of cooperation between a colonialist power and the Jewish people.

However, it was the events of 1831-40 that paved the way for the establishment of a Jewish state in Palestine. Lord Palmerston, the British Foreign Secretary in 1840-41, proposed establishing a British protectorate in the Ottoman Empire, to be settled by Jews as a buffer area – an obstacle to Mohammed Ali of Egypt and to political unity in the Arab regions.

Britain launched a new policy supporting Jewish settlement in Palestine after Eastern European Jews, particularly those in Czarist Russia, whose living conditions were poor in any case, suffered cruel persecution. Consequently, with the rise of nationalism, Zionism appeared as a drastic international solution to the Jewish problem, transforming the Jewish religion into a nationalist attachment to a special Jewish homeland and a special Jewish state. Other factors influencing the birth and development of the Zionist movement were the increasingly competitive interests shared by European colonialists in Africa and Asia, and the Zionist colonialist movement for control of Palestine.

British imperialism found in Zionism a perfect tool for attaining its own interests in the Arab East, which was strategically and economically important for the Empire. Likewise, Zionism used British colonialist aspirations to gain international backing and economic resources for its project of establishing a Jewish national home in Palestine.

This alliance of British imperialism and Zionism resulted in the birth of what is known in history books as the Balfour Declaration (November 2, 1917). It is a conspicuous example of the British policy of seizing another nation's land and resources and effacing its identity. It is a policy based on aggression, expansion and repression of a native people's aspirations for national liberation.

For the Palestinians, the year 1917 was the first of many – 1920, 1921, 1929, 1936, 1948, 1967, 1987, 2002 – marked by tragedy, war, disaster, killing, destruction, homelessness and catastrophe.

Imperialist Britain called for a higher committee of seven European countries. The report submitted in 1907 to British Prime Minister Sir Henry Campbell-Bannerman emphasized that the Arab countries and the Muslim-Arab people living in the Ottoman Empire presented a very real threat to European countries, and it recommended the following actions:

> to promote disintegration, division and separation in the region

> to establish artificial political entities that would be under the authority of the imperialist countries

> to fight any kind of unity – whether intellectual, religious or historical – and taking practical measures to divide the region's inhabitants

> to establish a buffer state in Palestine, populated by a strong, foreign presence which would be hostile to its neighbours and friendly to European countries and their interests

Doubtless the recommendations of Campbell-Bannerman's higher committee paved the way for the Jews in Palestine. It gave British approval to the Zionist movement's policy of separating Palestine from the Arab lands in order to establish an imperialist core that would insure foreign influence in the region.

Jewish imperialist projects in Palestine followed in quick succession. World War I, 1914-1918, was a critically important period for Zionist and British imperialist policies for Palestine. Included in an exchange of letters between Sharif Hussein of Mecca and Sir Henry McMahon was the Damascus Protocol (July 14, 1915.) Sharif Hussein indicated to McMahon the boundaries of the Arab countries

163

in Asia to which Britain would grant independence – the Arabian Peninsula, Iraq/ Mesopotamia, Syria and southern parts of present-day Turkey. He excluded Aden because it was a British military base.

In May 1916, Britain and France signed a secret document – the Sykes-Picot Agreement – to divide the Arab East at a time when Britain was exchanging letters with Sharif Hussein about recognising the independence of the region. In the agreement, Britain and France pledged to divide the Ottoman Empire as follows:

[A map in the original]

1. The Lebanese and Syrian coasts were given to France.

2. South and Central Iraq were given to Britain.

3. An international administration was created in Palestine excluding the two ports of Haifa and Acre.

4. A French zone of influence, including eastern Syria and Mosul province.

5. Transjordan and the northern part of Baghdad province were made a British zone of influence.

Notes on Contributors

Sami Adwan is Professor of Education at Bethlehem University and co-Director of PRIME. A schools consultant in Bethlehem District, he has published on the Palestinian education system, teachers, and particularly schoolbooks. With Dan Bar-On he was awarded the Alexander Peace Prize (2001) and the Vic Goldberg Prize (2005) for work on Peace in the Middle East.

Dan Bar-On is Professor of Psychology at Ben-Gurion University, where he holds the *David Lopatie Chair for Post-Holocaust Psychological Studies.* He is the co-director of PRIME (Peace Research Institute in the Middle East) with Sami Adwan. Books include *The Indescribable and the Undiscussable* (1999). He was awarded the Eric Maria Remarque Peace Prize (2003).

Lars Berggren is Associate Professor at the Department of History, Lund University, Sweden. Mainly a social historian, he has worked on history didactics, such as the evaluation of history teaching in compulsory school, with Roger Johansson. He has also been engaged in initial teacher-training at Malmö School of Education.

Luigi Cajani teaches Modern History at the Facoltà di Scienze Umanistiche of the Università La Sapienza, in Rome, and History Didactics at the SSIS (Initial Teacher Training Postgraduate School) of Lazio. His research fields are history didactics, the history of crime and criminal justice in Italy during the Ancien Régime and German-Italian relations during World War II. He has participated in many European projects in history didactics. He coordinated the Italian Ministry of Education committee on history, geography and social sciences curricula for first-level school. He is Vice-President of the International Society for History Didactics and member of the Wissenschaftlicher Ausschuß of the Georg-Eckert-Institut für internationale Schulbuchforscuhng in Braunschweig (Germany).

María Jesús Cava Mesa is Professor of Contemporary History and History of International Relations at the Faculty of Arts, University of Deusto (Bilbao). She directs the Department of History and Cliohnet and coordinates the CliohRES Excellence Network. She publishes on aspects of contemporary history. Recent books and articles include *Bilbao Chamber of Commerce: More than 100 years of history* (2003), *Histories of Bilbao, 1875-1914* (2005), *SVRNE 1905-2005* (2005) and *Spanish and Basque Nationalism* (2002).

Roger Johansson is a senior lecturer in History in the Teacher Education department at Malmö University, Sweden. His dissertation (2001) was *The Struggle over the History – Adalen 1931.* He is a visiting scholar at Michigan State University and is currently researching on May Day – modernization, social conflicts, and the use of history.

Mary Koutselini is Associated Professor of Curriculum Development and Evaluation at the University of Cyprus, where she specialises in curriculum development, teaching and teacher education, particularly the promotion of quality in education and the development of Citizenship Education. Her publications in the field include contributions to CiCe publications and to the IEA research on Civic Education.

Cătălina Mihalache is a researcher at A. D. Xenopol History Institute (Iasi), the Institute for International Research of Schoolbooks in Braunschweig, the Open Society Archive (Budapesta), and the Süd Ost Institute of München. Previously she taught history in a technical school in Iaşi. Her research areas include the recent history of education, memory studies, textbooks and historiography, public and unprofessional uses of historical knowledge.

Mirela-Luminiţa Murgescu is Associate Professor at the Faculty of History, University of Bucharest. She has participated in international projects on textbook analysis, nationalism, social and cultural history. Among her publications are *Nations and States in Southeast Europe, Între 'bunul creştin' şi 'bravul român' (1831-1878)* [Between the 'Good Christian' and the 'Brave Romanian' and

Istoria din ghiozdan. Memorie şi manuale şcolare în România anilor 1990 [History from the school bag. Memory and schoolbooks in Romania during the 1990s].

Concepción Maiztegui Oñate is a senior lecturer in the Department of Education, University of Deusto, Bilbao (Spain). Her main research interest is focused around the areas of participation and community development, with special attention to the empowerment process, linked to socio-educational policies. She has conducted several intervention studies with different target groups at local level, and is a member of CiCe and the European Excellence Network on International Migration, Integration and Social Cohesion.

Panayota Papoulia-Tzelepi was Professor of Education in the University of Patras, Greece. She was Vice-President of the Greek Pedagogical Institute in the Hellenic Ministry of Education between 2001 and 2004, responsible for the production of new textbooks in secondary education. She was a member of the CiCe Steering Group (1998-2002) and subsequently a member of the CiCe MA development team.

Julia A Spinthourakis specialises in multilingual and multicultural education in the University of Patras. A former secondary education history and social studies teacher, her area of specialisation is Multilingual/Multicultural Education and her publications concern linguistically and culturally-differentiated populations, teacher education, their beliefs and the role of culture in communication and the classroom. She is a member of the CiCe Executive (2005-2008).

Nicole Tutiaux-Guillon is *Professeuse des universités* (professor) in the IUFM of Lille. *Agrégée Docteur* (PhD) in history didactics and accredited research supervisor (*habilitation à diriger des recherches*), she has participated in European and international projects on history/geography and citizenship. Present research focuses on effective teaching and learning and on social, civic and ethical goals of history/geography teaching.

Alistair Ross is Professor of Education at London Metropolitan University, where he directs the Institute for Policy Studies in Education. He coordinates the Children's Identity and Citizenship in

Europe Erasmus Thematic network. His research interests are in children's social and political learning, teachers and their careers, and access to higher education.

Jörn Rüsen is President of the Institute for Advanced Study in the Humanities at Essen and Professor of History and Historical Culture at the University of Witten/Herdecke.. His research includes the theory and methodology of history, modern intellectual history and historical consciousness. Recent books include *Zerbrechende Zeit* (2001) and *New Ways of Historical Thinking* (2005).

References

Adwan, S and Firer, R. (1999) *The Narrative of the 1967 war in the Israeli and Palestinian History and Civics Textbooks and Curricula Statement.* Braunschweig: Eckert Institute

Adwan, S. and Bar On, D. (2000) *The Role of Non-Governmental Organizations in Peace Building Between Palestinians and Israelis.* Beit Jala, Palestine: PRIME

Adwan, S. and Bar On, D. (2001) *Victimhood and Beyond.* Beit Jala/Palestine: PRIME

Adwan, S. and Bar-On, D. (2002) *Sharing each other's Historical narratives: Palestinians and Israelis* [first booklet] Beit Jalal Palestine: PRIME. [available in Arabic, Hebrew, English, French, Spanish and Italian]

Adwan, S. and Firer, R. (1997) *The Narrative of Palestinian Refugees During the War of 1948 in Israeli and Palestinian History and Civic Education Textbooks.* Paris: UNESCO

Aftonbladet (2004) 26 December

Aftonbladet (2005) 14 February

Alahiotis, S, and Karatzia-Stavlioti, E. (2006) Effective curriculum policy and cross-curricularity: Analysis of the new curriculum design of the Hellenic Pedagogical Institute. *Pedagogy Culture and Society* 2, forthcoming

Alahiotis, S. (2004) Towards a modern educational system: Cross-curricularity and Flexible Zone change education and improve its quality [in Greek]. in Aggelides, P. and G. Mavroides, (eds) *Educational innovations for the school of tomorrow*, Athens: Tipothito, G. Dardanos

Albacete, C., Cárdenas, I. and Delgado, C. (2000) *Enseñar y aprender la democracia.* Barcelona: Síntesis.

Allardyce, G. (1990) Toward World History: American Historians and the Coming of the World History Course. *Journal of World History*, 1/1, 23 – 76

Almas, D., Fotescu, E. (1985) *Istoria Patriei. Manual pentru clasa a IV-a*, Bucureşti: Editura Didactică şi Pedagogică

Alvarez Junco, J (1998) ¿Modernidad o atraso? Sociedad, cultura y política. En: S. Juliá (coord), *Debates en torno al 98:Estado, Sociedad y Política.* Madrid: Comunidad de Madrid

Alvarez, M. (2002) El experto en educación. Formación y desarrollo profesional en el marco europeo en C. Maiztegui y R. Santibáñez. *El perfil del educador social y el pedagogo.* Bilbao: Universidad de Deusto.

Anaut, L. (2002) *Valores escolares y educación para la ciudadanía.* Barcelona: Grao

Ankersmit, F. R. (2001) The Sublime Dissociation of the Past: Or how to be(come) what one is no longer, *History and Theory* 40, 295-323

Apple, M. (1993) *Official Knowledge.* New York NY: Routledge

Argibai, M., Celorio, G and Celorio, J. (1991) *La cara oculta de los textos escolares.* Investigación curricular en Ciencias Sociales. Bilbao: Hegoa

Aristotle (1992) *The Politics* (trans Trevor J. Saunders, T. A. Sinclair) Harmondsworth: Penguin Classics

Asociación para la Enseñanza de la Historia (1998) *La reforma de los programas de Historia.* (Available: http://mimosa.pntic.mec.es/~mgarciaa/debates/deb_2.htm)

Assmann, A. and Frevert, U. (1999) *Geschichtsvergessenheit – Geschichtsversessenheit. Vom Umgang mit deutschen Vergangenheiten nach 1945.* Stuttgart

Assmann, J. (1992) *Das kulturelle Gedächtnis. Schrift, Erinnerung und politische Identität in frühen Hochkulturen.* München: C.H. Beck

Assmann, J. (1995) Collective Memory and Cultural Identity, in: *New German Critique,* 65, 125-133

Audigier, F. (1993) *Les représentations que les élèves ont de l'histoire et de la géographie, à la recherche des modèles disciplinaires, entre leur définition par l'institution et leur appropriation par les élèves.* PhD Thesis. Paris: Université Paris 7 – Denis Diderot

Audigier, F. (1996) *Recherches de didactiques de l'histoire, de la géographie, de l'éducation civique, un itinéraire pour contribuer à la construction d'un domaine de recherche,* Habilitation Thesis, Paris: Université Paris 7 – Denis Diderot

Audigier, F. (1998) *Contributions à l'étude de la causalité et des productions des élèves dans l'enseignement de l'histoire et de la géographie.* Paris: INRP

Audigier, F. (2003) Histoire, géographie, éducation civique: trois disciplines déstabilisées pour une citoyenneté en mutation, in Derouet, J.C. (ed), *Le collège unique en question.* Paris: PUF

Audigier, F., Crémieux, C. and Mousseau, M.-J. (1996) *L'enseignement de l'histoire et de la géographie en troisième et en seconde, étude descriptive et comparative.* Paris: INRP

Balado, M. (2003) *La Constitución Española de 1978 en su XXV aniversario: una obra antológica.* Madrid: Ed. Bosch

Banks, J. (1997) *Educating citizens in a multicultural society.* New York: Teachers' College Press, Columbia University

Barrère, A. (2002) *Les enseignants au travail, routines incertaines.* Paris: l'Harmattan

Bartolomé Pina, M. (ed) (2002) *Identidad y ciudadanía. Un reto para la educación intercultural.* Madrid: Narcea

Bastida, A. (1994) *Desaprender la guerra. Una visión crítica de la educación para la paz.* Barcelona: Icaria

Bauberot, J. (1997) *La morale laïque contre l'ordre moral.* Paris: Seuil

Bauman, Z. (2004) *Identity: Conversations with Benedetto Vecchi.* Cambridge: Polity Press

Becher, U. A. J. and Riemenschneider, R. (eds) (2000) *Internationale Verständigung. 25 Jahre Georg-Eckert-Institut für internationale Schulbuchforschung in Braunschweig.* Hannover: Verlag Hahnsche Buchhandlung

Bentley, J. (2005) Myths, wagers and some moral implications of world history. *Journal of World History,* 16/1, 51-82

Berggren, L. and Johansson, R. (2005) *Nationella utvärderingen av skolämnet Historia i grundskolan – en preliminär skiss.* Malmö: Malmö högskola

Bergmann, K. (1982) Imperialistische Tendenzen in Geschichtsdidaktik und Geschichtsunterricht ab 1890, in Bergmann, K. and Schneider, G. (eds), *Gesellschaft Staat Unterricht. Beiträge zu einer Geschichte der Geschichtsdidaktik und des Geschichtsunterrichts von 1500-1980.* Düsseldorf: Pädagogischer Verlag Schwann

Borne, D. (1995) Communauté de mémoire et rigueur critique, *Autrement*, 150 -151 (Passés recomposés, champs et chantiers de l'histoire) 125-133

Borries, B. von, Pandel, H-J, Rüsen, J. (eds) (1991) *Geschichtsbewußtsein empirisch* (Geschichtsdidaktik, Studien, Materialien. Neue Folge, Bd. 7). Pfaffenweiler: Centaurus

Bozgan, O., Lazar, L., Stamatescu, M., Teodorescu, B. (1999) *Istorie. Manual pentru clasa a XII-a*, Bucureşti: Editura All Educaţional

Brezeanu, S., Cioroianu, A., Müller, F., Radulescu, M., Retegan, M.(2000) *Istoria Romanilor. Manual pentru clasa a XII-a*, Bucureşti: Editura RAO Educational

Broschyr om Riket (2004) Malmö: Malmö museer

Bruter, A. (1997) *L'histoire enseignée au Grand Siècle*. Paris: Belin

Bryld, C. (1999) *At formidle historie – Vilkår, kendtegn, formål*. Roskilde: Roskilde Universitetsforlag

Burlec, L., Lazar, L., Teodorescu, B. (1997) *Istoria Românilor. Manual pentru clasa a IV-a*, Bucureşti, Editura All

Cajani, L. (2002) A World History curriculum for the Italian school. *World History Bulletin*, XVIII, 2, 26-32

Carr, David (1984) Time-consciousness and historical consciousness, in: Cho, K.K. (Ed.), *Philosophy and science in phenomenological perspective*, Dordrecht, Boston, Lancaster, 31-44

Carr, David (1986) *Time, Narrative and History*. Studies in Phenomenolgy and Existential Philosophy. Bloomington: Indiana UP

Carras, C. (2001) Preface. In C. Koulouri (ed) *Teaching the History of Southeastern Europe*. Thessaloniki: Centre of Democracy and Reconciliation in Europe. Southeast European Joint History Project

Carras, C. (2002) Preface, in C. Koulouri (ed) *Clio in the Balkans. The Politics of History Education*, Thessaloniki

Cârtănă, I., Dondorici, G., Lica, E., Osanu, O., Poamă, E., Stoica R, (2000) *Istoria românilor. Manual pentru clasa a XII-a*, Piteşti: Carminis

Castells, M. (2001) *The Internet Galaxy. Reflections on the Internet, Business, and Society*. Oxford, New York: Oxford University Press

Cerini, G. and Fiorin I. (eds) (2001) *I curricoli della scuola di base. Testi e commenti*. Napoli: Tecnodid (in collaborazione con Zanichelli Editore)

Chaitin, J, Obeidi, F. Adwan, S and Bar-On, D. (2004) *The Role of Palestinian and Israeli Environmental NGOs in Peace Building*. Beit Jala, Palestine: PRIME

Chervel, A. (1998) *La culture scolaire*. Paris: Belin

Clerc, P. (2002) *La culture scolaire du lycée en géographie, le monde à l'école*. Rennes: PUR

Cogan, J. and Derricott, R. (1998) *Citizenship for the 21st Century. An international Perspective on Education*. London: Kogan Page

Colomb, J. (ed) (1999) *Un transfert de connaissances des résultats d'une recherche à la définition de contenus de formation en didactique*. Paris: INRP

Commission of the European Community (1995) Commission Communication COM (95) 567 The external Dimension of the EU's Human Rights Policy: From Rome to Maastricht and beyond (22-11-1995) Brussels: European Community

Condorcet [Marie Jean Antoine Nicolas Caritat, Marquis de Condorcet] (1792) *Projet sur l'organisation générale de l'instruction publique*

171

Cortina, A. (1999) *Ciudadanos del mundo. Hacía una teoría de la ciudadanía.* Madrid: Alianza Editorial

Cortina, A. and Conill, J. (eds) (2001) *Educar en la ciudadanía.* Valencia: Colección Pensamiento y Sociedad. Institució Alfons el Magnànim.

Council of Europe (1999) *Lessons in history: The Council of Europe and the teaching of history.* Council of Europe Publishing

Council of Europe (1999) *Towards a plural and tolerant approach to teaching history: A range of sources and new didactics*

Council of Europe (2000a) *The misuses of history*

Council of Europe (2000b) *Teaching 20th century history*

Council of Europe (2001) *Stocktaking research on policies for education for democratic citizenship and management diversity in Southeast Europe.* Strasbourg: Task Force on Education and Youth and Council of Europe

Cristescu, O., Pasaila, V., Teodorescu, B., Tomi, R, (1993) *Istoria Românilor. Epoca modernă și contemporană. Manual pentru clasa a VIII-a,* București, Editura Didactica si Pedagogica

CronoX (2005) Call of Duty 2. *Monumentul eroului necunoscut,* Level 6

Curriculum naţional (1999) *Programe şcolare pentru clasele a IX-a. Vol. III. Ariile curriculare: Om şi societate, arte, tehnologii, educaţie fizică şi sport,* Bucureşti

Curriculum naţional (1999) *Programe şcolare pentru clasele a V-a -a VIII-a. Aria curriculară Om şi societate,* Bucureşti: Debate

Delgado, C. (2004) La formación de los ciudadanos en la enseñanza obligatoria. Una propuesta didáctica. Iber. *Didáctica de las Ciencias Sociales, Geografía e Historia, 44.* 36-44

Delors, J. (1996) *Education: Learning the treasure within.* Paris: Unesco

Denier O. (2002) L'épreuve d'étude de documents d'histoire au baccalauréat général, in *La Revue de l'enseignement de l'histoire, de la géographie, de l'éducation civique.* Clermont-Ferrand: CRDP d'Auvergne, 45-54

Departamento de Educación, Universidades e Investigación (2004) *Programas de innovación educativa 2003-2006.* Vitoria-Gasteiz: Gobierno Vasco

Douzant-Rosenfeld, D. (1993) Géographie et professeurs du second degré. Le grand écart , in Dory, D., Douzant-Rozenfeld, D. and Knafou, R., *Matériaux pour une sociologie de la géographie.* Paris: L'Harmattan

Dragona, T. and Frangoudaki, A. (2001) The persistence of ethnocentric school history. In C. Koulouri (Ed.) *Teaching the history of Southeastern Europe.* Thessaloniki: Centre for Democracy and Reconciliation in Southeast Europe

Dumitrescu N., Manea, M., Nita, C., Pascu, A., Trandafir, A., Trandafir, M. (1999) *Istoria Românilor. Manual pentru clasa a XII-a,* Bucureşti: Humanitas

European Commission (2001) *Communication from the Commission on Conflict Prevention* (11-4-2001) Brussels: European Community

European Council, Official Journal C325 (2002) *Treaty establishing European Union* (24-12-2002) Brussels: European Community

Eurydice (2004) Citizenship education in schools in Europe. (<http://www.eurydice.org/Search/frameset_en.html>)

Expressen (2005) 14 February

Ferro, M. (1984) *The use and abuse of history, or, How the past is taught.* London; Boston: Routledge and Kegan Paul (first published Paris: Payot, 1981)

Firer, R. and Adwan S. (2004) *The Israeli-Palestinian Conflict in History and Civic Textbooks of Both Nations*. Hannover: Verlag Hahnsche Buchhandlung

Frey, K. (1994) *Die Projektmethode*. 5th ed. Weinheim: Beltz.

Friedländer, S. (1994) Trauma, Memory, and Transference, in: Hartman, Geoffrey H. (Ed.): *Holocaust Remembrance: the Shapes of Memory,* Oxford, Cambridge (Blackwell), 252-263

Friedländer, S. (1998) Writing the history of the Shoa: Some major dilemmas, in: Blanke, H-W., Jaeger, F. and Sandkühler, T. (eds) *Dimensionen der Historik. Geschichtstheorie, Wissenschaftsgeschichte und Geschichtskultur heute.* Jörn Rüsen zum 60. Geburtstag. Köln: Böhlau, 407-414

Furay, C. and Salevouris, M. (2000) *The methods and skills of history: A practical guide* (2nd Edition). Illinois: Harlan Davidson

GADs historieleksikon (2003) Copenhagen: GADs forlag

García Garrido, J. L. (1987) *Sistemas educativos de hoy*. Madrid: Ed. Dykinson

Garcia, P. and Leduc, J. (2003) *L'enseignement de l'histoire en France de l'Ancien Régime à nos jours.* Paris: Armand Colin

Gazi, E. (2004) The transformation of ethnic state. *To Vima*, 14 November, [in Greek]

Geary, P. J. (2002) *The Myth of Nations. The Medieval Origins of Europe.* Princeton and Oxford: Princeton University Press

Georgiadis, N. (2005) Trends in State Education Policy in Greece: 1976 to 1997 Reform, *Education Policy Analysis Archives*, Vol. 13, No. 9, http://epaa.asu.edu/epaa/v13n9/. Retrieved: 27/03/2005.

Giesen, B. (2000) National Identity as Trauma: The German Case, in: Strath, B. (ed) *Myth and Memory in the Construction of Community: Historical Patterns in Europe and beyond.* Brüssel: Lang, 227-247

Gimeno Sacristán, J. (2003) Volver a leer la educación desde la ciudadanía. En J.Martínez Bonafé (coord.). *Ciudadanía, poder y educación*, 11-34. Barcelona: Graó

Gómez, E. (2005) Tendencias en la educación ciudadana del siglo XXI. *Iber. Didáctica de las Ciencias Sociales, Geografía e Historia, 44,* 7-15

Greece, Ministry of Education and Religious Affairs. (2003). *Curriculum for obligatory Education Presidential Decree* [in Greek]. FEK B, 303, 13-03-2003 (http://www.pi-schools.gr).

Grigore, S., Berciu-Draghicescu, A., Cristea, N. (2000) *Istoria românilor. Manual pentru clasa a IV-a,* Bucureşti: Editura Sigma

Habermas, J. (1992) *Teoría de la acción comunicativa*. Taurus. Madrid

Halbwachs, M. (1980) *The collective memory.* New York

Halbwachs, M. (1992) *On Collective Memory,* Chicago: The University of Chicago Press

Heidegger, M. (1980) *Sein und Zeit*. Tübingen

Hery, E. (1999) *Un siècle de leçons d'histoire, l'histoire enseignée au lycée, 1870-1970.* Rennes: Presses Universitaires de Rennes

Högberg, A. and Kihlström, H. (eds) (2005) *Medeltid på tevetid: en dokusåpas historiedidaktik.* Mälmo: Mälmo Kulturmiljö and Mälmo Museer

http://svt.se/svt/jsp/Crosslink.jsp?d=23133

http://svt.se/svt/jsp/Crosslink.jsp?d=23166

Hurezeanu, E., Smarandache, G., Totu, M. (1988) *Istoria modernă a României. Manual pentru clasa a IX-a,* Bucureşti: Editura Didactică şi Pedagogică

Husbands, C. (1992) Facing the facts: History in schools and the curriculum, in P. Black (ed) *Education: Putting the records straight.* Stafford: Network Educational Press

Husbands, C. (1996) *What is history teaching? Language, ideas and meaning in learning about the past.* London: Open University Press

INRP (1989) *Supports informatifs et documents dans l'enseignement de l'histoire et de la géographie, Rapports de recherches,* 11. Paris: INRP

Jeismann, K-E. (1985) *Geschichte als Horizont der Gegenwart. Über den Zusammenhang von Vergangenheitsdeutung, Gegenwartsverständnis und Zukunftsperspektive.* Paderborn

Jenkins, K. (1996) *What is history?* London: Routledge

Jensen, B. E. (2003) *Historie – livsverden og fag.* København: Gyldendal

Juliá, S. (1998) Retóricas de muerte y resurrección: los intelectuales en la crisis de conciencia nacional. En: Comunidad de Madrid (ed) *Debates en torno al 98: Estado, Sociedad y Política.* Madrid: Comunidad de Madrid

Kalaitzidis, P. (2003) Orthodoxy and Greek identity [in Greek] *Indiktos,* 17, 44-94 [in Greek] Kalouris

Karahassan, H. and Zembylas, M. (2006) The politics of memory and forgetting in history textbooks: towards a pedagogy of reconciliation and peace in a divided Cyprus. In Ross, A. (ed) *Citizenship Education: Europe and the World.* London: CiCe

Karlsson, K-G. (1999) *Historia som vapen,* Stockholm: Natur och kultur

Kelpanides, M. (2005) Ideology in school textbooks: The continuous idealization of bolshevism and the falsification of history in a textbook of secondary school [in Greek]. *Sciences of Education,* 2, 181-203

Kennedy, K. J. (1991) The Historical perspective: the contribution of history to citizenship education. in R. Groos and T. Dynneson (eds) *Social Science Perspectives on Citizenship Education.* New York: Teachers' College Press

Kerr, D. (1999) *Citizenship education: an international comparison.* (ww.inca.org.Link/thematic.asp)

Kerr, D. (1999). *Citizenship Education: an International Comparison.* Slough: NFER

Kitromilides, P. (1998) On the intellectual content of Greek nationalism: Paparrigopoulos, Byzantium and the Great Idea. in D. Ricks and P. Magdalino (eds) *Byzantium and the modern Greek identity.* London: Centre for Hellenic Studies, King's College

Kölbl, C. (2004) *Geschichtsbewußtsein im Jugendalter. Grundzüge einer Entwicklungspsychologie historischer Sinnbildung.* Bielefeld: Transcript

Koulouri, C. (2001) *Teaching the History of Southeastern Europe,* Thessaloniki: Center for Democracy and Reconciliation in Southeast Europe

Koulouri, C. (2002) Introduction in C. Koulouri (ed) *Clio in the Balkans. The politics of history education.* Thessaloniki: Centre for Democracy and reconciliation in Southeast Europe

Koutselini, M. (1997a) Curriculum as political text: the case of Cyprus (1935-1990). *History of Education,* 26, 4, 395-407

Koutselini, M (1997b) *Educational policy and the teaching of Ancient Greek.* Athens: Gregoris [in Greek]

Koutselini, M. (2000) Citizenship Education in context: The role of professional collaboration for citizenship in Europe. in Ross, A. (ed) *Developing Identities in Europe: citizenship education and higher education.* London: CiCe, 101-109

Koutselini, M. and Maratheftis, M. (2000). *The function and the curricula of the pedagogical Academy of Cyprus.* Nicosia: mimeo [in Greek]

Koutselini, M. and Papanastasiou, C. (1997) Civic education in Cyprus- Issues in focus: A curriculum research study. *Children's Social and Economics Education.* 2, 3, 113-129

Kursplaner för grundskolan, Stockholm: Skolverket (http://www3.skolverket.se/ki/eng/comp)

LaCapra, D. (1994) *History, Theory, Trauma: Representing the Holocaust.* Ithaca: Cornell University Press

LaCapra, D. (1997) Revisiting the Historians' Debate. Mourning and Genocide, in: Ne'Emanarad G, (ed) Passing into History: Nazism and the Holocaust beyond Memory. In honour of Saul Friedländer on his 65th Birthday. *History and Memory,* 9, 1-2, Fall, 80-112

LaCapra, D. (2001) *Writing history, writing trauma.* Baltimore: The Johns Hopkins University Press

Laliotou, I. (2004) *Transatlantic Subjects: Acts of Migration and Cultures of Transnationalism between Greece and America.* Chicago: University of Chicago Press

Laurie, S.S. (1900) Instruction in History and Citizenship. *Parents' Review,* XI:1-8, 69-77. http://www.amblesideonline.org/PR/PR11p001HistoryCitizenship.shtml (Retrieved 10/01/06)

Lautier, N. (1997) *À la rencontre de l'histoire.* Lille: Presses universitaires du septentrion

Lautier, N. (2001) *Psychosociologie de l'éducation.* Paris: A. Colin

Laville, C. (2001) Historical consciousness and history education: what to expect from the first for the second, paper presented at the Canadian Historical Consciousness in International Context Conference, UBC, Vancouver, http://pkp.ubc.ca/harvester/oai/viewrecord

Lavisse, E. (1885) *L'enseignement de l'histoire à l'école primaire, in Questions d'enseignement national.* Paris: Librairie Classique Armand Colin

Lazar L. and Lupu, V. (2001) *Istoria Românilor. Manual pentru clasa a VIII-a*, Bucuresti: Editura Teora

Lenoir, Y. (2000) La recherche dans le champ des didactiques: quelques remarques sur les types de recherche, leur pertinence et leurs limites pour la formation à l'enseignement, *Revue suisse des sciences de l'éducation*, 1/2000, 177-220

Liebsch, B. and Rüsen, J. (eds) (2001) *Trauer und Geschichte.* (Beiträge zur Geschichtskultur, Bd. 22). Köln: Böhlau

Lopes Don, P. (2003) Establishing World History as a Teaching Field: Comments from the Field. *The History Teacher*, 36, 4, 505-525

Malmö Maseer (2004) *Riket: glimpses of history.* Malmö: Museer

Manea, M., Pascu, A., Teodorescu B. (1992) *Istoria românilor. Din cele mai vechi timpuri până la revoluţia din 1821. Manual pentru clasa a XI-a*, Bucureşti: Editura Didactică şi Pedagogică

Manea, M., Teodorescu, B. (1994) *Istoria românilor. Epoca modernă şi contemporană,* Bucureşti: Editura Didactică şi Pedagogică

Manning, P. (2003) *Navigating world history: Historians create a global past.* New York: Palgrave

Marchesi, A. and Martín, E. (2002) *Evaluación de la educación secundaria. Fotografía de una etapa polémica.* Madrid: Fundación Santa María

Marshall, T. H. (1950) *Citizenship and Social Class* (1950)

Megill, A. (1998) History, Memory, Identity, in *History of the Human Sciences* 11 37-62

Ministerio de Educación (2004) Una educación de calidad para todos y entre todos en (<http://debateeducativo.mec.es/>)

Ministry of Education [Cyprus] (*Ipourgio Pedias*) (1991) *Civics for the second grade of Lyceum.* Nicosia: Ministry of Education

Ministry of Education [Cyprus] (*Ipourgio Pedias*) (1993) *Becoming a Good Citizen* (for the sixth grade) Nicosia: Ministry of Education

Ministry of Education [Cyprus] (*Ipourgio Pedias*) (1994a) *Primary School Curriculum.* Nicosia: Ministry of Education

Ministry of Education [Cyprus] (*Ipourgio Pedias*) (1994b) *Becoming a Good Citizen* (for the fifth grade). Nicosia: Ministry of Education

Ministry of Education and Culture [Cyprus] (*Ipourgio Pedias kai politismou*) (2004a) *National Report.* Nicosia: Ministry of Education and Culture

Ministry of Education and Culture [Cyprus] (*Ipourgio Pedias kai politismou*) (2004b): *Democratic and Humanistic Education in the Euro-Cypriot Society. The Report of the Reform Committee,* August 2004. Nicosia [in Greek]

Mitchell, J. and Quan. K. (2001) Service learning and Conflict Resolution Education. OJPCR: *The online Journal of Peace and Conflict Resolution,* 4, 1, Summer 2001

Mitu, S. (ed) (1999) *Istorie. Manual pentru clasa a XII-a,* Bucuresti: Sigma

Mitu, S. (ed) 2nd ed. (2000) *Istorie. Manual pentru clasa a XII-a,* Bucuresti: Sigma

Mozes Kor, E. (2004) Echoes from Auschwitz: My journey to healing, in Kulturwissen-schaftliches Institut (ed) *Jahrbuch 2002/03,* Bielefeld: Transcript, 262-270

Müller, K. E. (1987) *Das magische Universum der Identität. Elementarformen sozialen Verhaltens.* Ein ethnologischer Grundriß. Frankfurt am Main

Müller, K. E. (2000) Ethnicity, Ethnozentrismus und Essentialismus, in: Eßbach, Wolfgang (ed) *Wir – Ihr, – Sie. Identität und Alterität in Theorie und Methode.* Würzburg, 317-343

Murgescu, M. (2004a) *Istoria din ghiozdan. Memorie și manuale școlare în Romania anilor 1990,* Bucuresti: Editura Dominor

Murgescu, M. (2004b) Memory in Romanian History, in M. Todorova (ed), *Balkan Identities. Nation and Memory,* London: Hurst and Co., 339-354.

National Centre for History in Schools (UCLA) (1996) Significance of history for the Educated Citizen. *National Standards for History, Grades 5-12.* http://nchs.ucla.edu/standards/dev-5-12a.html (Retrieved: 10/4/2005)

National Standards for History (1996) Los Angeles: National Centre for History in the Schools

Naval, C. and Laspalas, J. (eds) (2000) *La educación cívica hoy. Una aproximación inter-disciplinar.* Pamplona: Eunsa

Neumann, E. (1985) *Tiefenpsychologie und neue Ethik.* Frankfurt am Main

Niethammer, Lutz (1992): *Posthistoire: has history come to an end?* London: Verso

Nora, P. (1989) Between Memory and History: Les Lieux de Mémoire, in *Representations* 26

Oane, S., Ochescu, M. (2001) *Istoria Românilor. Manual pentru clasa a VIII-a,* Bucuresti: Humanitas

Ochescu, Maria; Oane, Sorin, (2001), *Istoria Românilor. Manual pentru clasa a IV-a,* Bucuresti: Teora

OECD (1994) *Lifelong learning for all.* Paris: OECD Publications

OECD (1998) *Making the curriculum work.* Paris: OECD Publications

Official Journal of the European Communities (2001): *Rec (2001)15, Teaching History for the 21st century.* Brussels: European Community

Official Journal of the European Communities (2004) *The School – a democratic learning community. The all – European study on Pupils' Participation in School* (26-4-2004). Brussels: European Community

Orain, O. (2000) Les postvidaliens et le plain-pied du monde. Pour une histoire de la géographie, in Levy, J. and Lussault, M. (ed) *Logiques de l'espace, esprit des lieux, géographies à Cerisy*. Paris: Belin

Pagès, J. (2005) Educación cívica, formación política y enseñanza de las ciencias sociales, de la geografía y de la historia. I*ber. Didáctica de las Ciencias Sociales, Geografía e Historia*, 44. 45-56

Panaitescu, P. P. (1990) *Istoria Românilor,* Bucureşti: Editura Didactică şi Pedagogică

Papanastasiou, C. and Koutselini, M. (1999) National Identity in the Civic Education of Cyprus, in: Torney-Purta, J. Schwille, and J. Amadeo (1999) *Civic Education Across countries: Twenty-four National Case Studies from the IEA Civic Education Project.* IEA, 161-178

Peck, C. (2005) New approaches to teaching history. *Canadian Social Studies*. 39 (2) http://www.quasar.ualberta.ca/css/Css_39_2/Editorial_39_2.htm (Retrieved: 10/1/06)

Peña, J. (2000) *La ciudadanía hoy: problemas y propuestas.* Valladolid: Universidad de Valladolid

Peña, J. (2001) *La formación histórica de la idea moderna de ciudadanía. Seminario: Historia y Naturaleza de la ciudadanía hoy.* Madrid: UNED

Pérez Ledesma, M. (ed) (2000) *Ciudadanía y democracia.* Madrid: Editorial Pablo Iglesias

Persianis, P. (1981) *The political and economic factors as the main determinants of educational policy in independent Cyprus (1960-1970).* Nicosia; mimeo

Petridis, T., Dragona, T. and Askouni N. (2001) The Southeast European History Project; The Turks in the Greek History textbooks. *Balkan Horizons*, 6, Winter: 14, 19

Pingel, F. (1995) *Befunde und Perspektiven – eine Zusammenfassung, in Pingel F. (ed), Macht Europa Schule? Die Darstellung Europas in Schulbüchern der Europäischen Gemeinschaft.* Frankfurt am Main: Diesterweg

Poirier, B. (ed) (1998) *Documents filmiques, documents écrits, étude comparée de leur statut et de leurs usages dans l'enseignement de l'histoire.* Paris: INRP

Procacci, G. (2005) *Carte d'identità. Revisionismi, nazionalismi e fondamentalismi nei manuali di storia.* Roma: Carocci

Proyecto ATLÁNTIDA. Educación y culturas democráticas. (http://www.proyecto-atlantida.org/)

Rawls, J. (1971) *Theory of Justice.* Massachusetts: Harvard University Press

Records of the Ministry of Education and Culture [Cyprus] (*Ipourgio Pedias kai politismou*) (2001) File 7.11.12.10.1: Teaching of Social Sciences. Nicosia: Ministry of Education and Culture

Relazione della Commissione mista storico-culturale italo-slovena (2000) I rapporti italosloveni 1880-1956. *Qualestoria*, XXVIII/2

Remy, R. (1998) *Handbook of citizenship competencies. Guidelines for comparing materials, assessing instruction and setting goals.* Alexandria (Vi): Association for Supervision and Curriculum Development.

Renoliet, J.-J. (1999) *L'UNESCO oubliée. La Société des Nation et la coopération intellectuelle (1919-1946).* Paris: Publications de la Sorbonne

Ricoeur, P. (1998) *Das Rätsel der Vergangenheit. Erinnern – Vergessen – Verzeihen* (Essener Kulturwissenschaftliche Vorträge, Bd. 2), Göttingen: Wallstein

Rodríguez, M. (2005) *La economía española del siglo XXVIII.* Barcelona: Liceus, Servicios de Gestión y Comunicación

Rosenzweig, R. and Thelen, D. (1998) *The Presence of the Past. Popular Uses of History in American Life,* New York: Columbia University Press

Ross, Alistair (2000) Introduction: Studying young people's constructions of identity in a changing Europe in: *Developing Identities in Europe: citizenship educational and higher education*. London: CiCe pp 1-11

Roth, M. S. (1995) *The Ironist's cage. Memory, Trauma, and the Construction of History*. New York: Columbia University Press

Rowe, J., (1990) To develop thinking citizens. *Educational Leadership*, 48 (3), 43-44

Rüsen, J. (1989) The Development of Narrative Competence in Historical Learning – An ontogenetical Hypothesis Concerning Moral Consciousness, in *History and Memory*. 1, 2, 35-60

Rüsen, J. (ed.) (2001) *Geschichtsbewußtsein. Psychologische Grundlagen, Entwicklungskonzepte, empirische Befunde*. (Beiträge zur Geschichtskultur, Bd. 21). Köln: Böhlau

Rüsen, J. (2002) Crisis, Trauma, and Identity (Chinese: Weiji, chuangshang yu rentong), in *Zhongguo xueshu* [China Scholarship] 3, 1, 15-38

Rüsen, J. (ed) (2002) *Western Historical Thinking: an intercultural debate*. New York: Berghahn books

Rüsen, J. (2004) Historical Thinking as Trauerarbeit. Burckhardt's Answer to a Question of Our Time, in Cesana, A. and Gossman, L. (eds) *Begegnungen mit Jacob Burckhardt (1818-1897)*. Beiträge zu Jacob Burckhardt, Bd. 4). Basel: Schwabe

Rüsen, J. (2004) How to overcome ethnocentrism? Approaches to a culture of recognition by history in the 21st century. *History and Theory* 43(4): 118-129

Santibañez, R. and Maiztegui, C. (2004) Equidad y abandono escolar: revisión de las principales investigaciones en esta área. In *Letras de Deusto, 34*, 165- 188

Sarremejane, P. (2001) *Histoire des didactiques disciplinaires*. Paris: l'Harmattan Sourp

Sato, M. (1996) Imagined Periperies. The World and its Peoples in Japanese Cartographic Imagination, in *Diogenes*, 173, 44/1, Spring, 119-145

Schröder, C. A. (1961) *Die Schulbuchverbesserung durch internationale geistige Zusammenarbeit*. Braunschweig: Georg Westermann Verlag

Scurtu, I., Curculescu, M., Dinca, C., Soare, A. (1999) *Istoria Românilor din cele mai vechi timpuri până astăzi*, Bucureşti: Editura Petrion

Scurtu, I., Curculescu, M., Dinca, C., Soare, A. 2nd ed (2000) *Istoria Românilor din cele mai vechi timpuri până astăzi*, Bucureşti: Editura Petrion

Sebba, J. (1997) *History for all*. London: Fulton Publishers

Slovensko-italijanski odnosi 1880-1956 (2001) *Poročilo slovensko – italijanske zgodovinsko – kulturne komisije (Koper – Capodistria, 25. julij 2000)*. Ljubljana: Nova revija

Sourp, R. (2002) Les mutations des formes de la causalité dans le raisonnement scolaire: l'exemple de la présentation de l'Europe classe de Quatrième, *L'information géographique*, 65, September, 3, 244-261

Southgate, B.C. (2000) *Why bother with history?* Harlow: Longman Press

Stearns, P.N., Seixas, P. and Wineburg, S. (eds) (2000). *Knowing, Teaching and Learning History: National and International Perspectives*, New York: New York University Press

Stradling, R. (2000) *Report Conference on The initial and in-service training of history teachers in South East Europe, Athens, Greece, 28 – 30 September 2000*. Strasbourg: Council for Europe (DCIV/EDU/HIST (2000) 07)

Straub, J. (2000) Identitätstheorie, Empirische Identitätsforschung und die Postmoderne Armchair Psychology, in *Zeitschrift für qualitative Bildungs-, Beratungs- und Sozialisationsforschung* 1

Straub, J. (2002) Multidisziplinäre Gedächtnisforschung revisited: Aleida Assmanns begriffliche Unterscheidungen und theoretische Integrationsbemühungen, in: *EuS* 13 (2002)

Svenska Dagbladet (2005) 5 February

Tempelhoff, J.W.N. (2003) Sedective roots to the past: Historical consciousness, memory and source mining for contemporary relevance, in Tempelhoff, J.W.N. (ed) *Historical consciousness and the future of our past*. Vanderbijlpark: Clio, 54-68

The Council of Europe (1995) *All Equal, All Different Educational pack*, Strasbourg: Council of Europe/European Youth Centre

The Council of Europe (1996) *ECRI, European Commission against racism and intolerance: ECRI general policy recommendation No 1: Combating racism, xenophobia, anti-Semitism and intolerance* (4-10-1996) Brussels: European Community

The teaching of history: new techniques, textbooks and the place of history in the curriculum (2000), Oslo: 19th International Congress of Historical Sciences.

Torney-Purta, J., and Schwille, J. (1986) Civic values learned in school: Policy and practice in industrialised countries. *Comparative Education Review*, 30, 30-49

Torney-Purta, J., Schwille, J. and Jo-Ann Amadeo (1999). *Civic Education across countries: Twenty-four national Case Studies from the IEA Civic Education Project*. Amsterdam: International Association for the Evaluation of Educational Achievement

Tuñón de Lara, M. (1986) *España: La quiebra de 1898*. Madrid: Sarpe

Tutiaux-Guillon, N. (1998) *L'enseignement et la compréhension de l'histoire sociale au collège et au lycée*. PhD Thesis, Université de Paris 7 – Denis Diderot. Published 2000, Parsis: Thèses à la carte, Villeneuve d'ascq

Tutiaux-Guillon, N. (ed) (2000) *L'Europe entre projet politique et objet scolaire*. Paris: INRP

Tutiaux-Guillon, N. (2004) *L'histoire-géographie dans le secondaire, analyses didactiques d'une inertie scolaire*, Habilitation Thesis. Lyon: Université Lumière-Lyon 2

Tutiaux-Guillon, N. et al (2005) *La prise en compte des finalités de l'enseignement de l'histoire et de la géographie par les enseignants du cycle 3 et du collège*. www.lyon.iufm.fr/recherche.html

Tutiaux-Guillon, N. and Mousseau, M. J. (1998) *Les jeunes et l'histoire, identités, valeurs, conscience historique*. Paris: INRP

Unamuno, M de (1914) Civilization is Civilism, in Mi *Religión y Otros Ensayos Breves 69*. Argentina: Espasa-Calpe: Argentina (1945)

van Beek, U. (2001) (ed) *Democracy under construction: Patterns from four countries*. Bloomfeild Hills, Opladen: Barbara Budrich

Valiente, C. (2000) Género y ciudadanía: los organismos de igualdad y el estado del bienestar. in M. Pérez Ledesma (ed) *Ciudadanía y democracia*. (p.199-230)

Vitanos, C. (2005) Didactica istoriei – educaţie pentru cetăţenia europeană, *Studii şi articole de istorie*, LXX, 173-178

Vulpe, A., Păun, R.,Băjenaru, R., Grosu, I. (2000) *Istoria românilor. Manual pentru clasa a VIII-a*, Bucureşti: Sigma

We and our neighbours. The majority and the minorities in the recent history textbooks in Romania, Bulgaria and Hungary (2004) Bucureşti: Humanitas

Wessnert, G. (2004) *Riket, boken om 1300-talet*. Stockholm: Sveriges Television

Winter, J. (1995) *Sights of Memory, Sights of Mourning. The Great War in European Cultural History*. Cambridge: University Press

Wolf, C. (1989) *Kindheitsmuster* (1976). Frankfurt am Main

Yannaras, C. (1986) *Philosophie sans rupture.* Geneva: Labor et Fides

Zamora, J. M. *et al,* (2001) *España: Sociedad, Política y Civilización, Siglos XIX-XX*

Index

181